THE
LITTLE BOOK OF
BIG
EXPLORATIONS

Other titles in the series

THE
LITTLE BOOK OF
BIG
EXPLORATIONS

Adventures into the Unknown That Changed Everything

JHENI OSMAN

Michael O'Mara Books Limited

First published in Great Britain in 2019
by Michael O'Mara Books Limited
9 Lion Yard
Tremadoc Road
London SW4 7NQ

A CIP catalogue record for this book is available from the British Library.

Papers used by Michael O'Mara Books Limited are natural, recyclable
products made from wood grown in sustainable forests.
The manufacturing processes conform to the environmental regulations
of the country of origin.

ISBN: 978-1-78929-079-0 in hardback print format
ISBN: 978-1-78929-175-9 in trade paperback print format
ISBN: 978-1-78929-080-6 in ebook format

1 2 3 4 5 6 7 8 9 10

www.mombooks.com

Designed and typeset by Ed Pickford
Illustrations by David Woodroffe

Printed and bound by CPI Group (UK) Ltd, Croydon, CR0 4YY

For Max and Dad, who also love to
explore this incredible planet.

CONTENTS

INTRODUCTION

Curiosity is innate in all of us. Without it, we would not have evolved into the technologically advanced species that we are today. Our insatiable appetite for knowledge has driven us to explore the unknown, pushing scientific, technical and geographical boundaries. And, while one person may gain the credit for going where no person has gone before, in reality there are many people working behind the scenes to enable such a feat. For example, when Neil Armstrong first set foot on the moon, it was the culmination of thousands of hours and different expertise that helped him take that giant leap for humankind. When Jacques Piccard and Don Walsh dived to the depths of Challenger Deep, a whole team of experts supported them at the surface 11 kilometres above. And Henry Walter Bates' decade-long adventures in the Amazon were possible only with the help of local guides and their knowledge.

Scientific discovery is the same. As Isaac Newton famously said: 'If I have seen further it is by standing on the shoulders of giants.' While a scientific breakthrough can come from the germ of an idea, years of observation and experimentation often follow before there is a paradigm shift in our knowledge. For example, Charles Darwin's voyage on HMS *Beagle* sowed the seeds for his ideas about how species evolve, but he took many years to pull together all his evidence before publishing his theory of evolution by natural selection. And, though it may be true that scientific breakthroughs are often made in the lab, sometimes it is only by voyaging to the final frontiers and physically exploring unknown worlds that groundbreaking discoveries can be made or verified.

This book focuses on the expeditions that have changed our understanding of science. So, while the likes of Marco Polo, Gertrude Bell and Edmund Hillary were great explorers, their expeditions are not included here as they didn't fundamentally contribute to our scientific understanding.

We can often get rather blasé about our forays into unknown worlds. For example, every day it seems that another space mission launches – nowadays to very little fanfare. It's so easy to forget just how challenging it must be to create a machine that will blast through the atmosphere, voyage millions of kilometres across the cosmos and slingshot into orbit around some alien world before touching down to explore the hostile environment and send back reams of data that continue to build on our knowledge of our cosmic neighbourhood and beyond. However, it's often said that we know more about space than we do about the oceans here on Planet Earth. It's certainly true that over the last few decades we have explored many of the extraordinary worlds that exist in our solar system, and yet only a handful of people have been to the deepest parts of our oceans. Experts estimate that 83 per cent of the world's land surface has now been transformed in some way by humans, but there remain pockets where few have ventured – areas of Papua New Guinea or the hostile wilderness of the Darién Gap between Panama and Colombia – and which remain ripe for scientific discovery.

From caves to mountains, the depths of the oceans to the outer reaches of space, many of these regions would be better left untouched by human hands. Yet, it's a fine balance: it is only through scientific exploration that humans and other species will be able to survive the environmental onslaught currently being wreaked upon this planet.

Historically, explorers tended to be from wealthy backgrounds. Today, while major expeditions still require funding and support, many of us are able to explore this incredible world for ourselves and contribute to scientific discovery. Through reading about great adventures that have changed our understanding of the world in which we live, maybe this book will inspire you to set off on your own journey of discovery – a journey that could also one day change the face of science.

PART 1

ADVENTURES IN UNKNOWN LANDS

Early human ancestors began migrating out of Africa possibly as far back as 2 million years ago. Travelling on land, they spread out across the globe – through the Arabian Peninsula and into the vast landmass of Eurasia. Not even a bitter ice age could stop these curious migrants, searching for a better life and new terrain to settle on. Fast forward a few millennia and intrepid explorers are still venturing across land on voyages of discovery, intent on learning more about every corner of our planet.

CLASSIFYING LIFE

A herd of reindeer saunter along the valley of rugged tundra that is cradled by snow-capped mountains. The low sun glints on the river, swollen by snowmelt. This is Lapland at its finest. Lines in hand, the men fish for their supper. Meals usually consist of smoked Arctic char or reindeer with a bit of bread made from pine bark, and a pudding of berries.

The team are almost halfway through their five-month trip, which started in the town of Uppsala, just north of Stockholm, then hugged the coast up to the remote realms of Lapland, taking the odd detour inland. Leading the group is the young botanist Carl Linnaeus, who will go on to become one of the most renowned scientists of his day and whose work helped lay the foundations of biological sciences.

Linnaeus was born in the village of Råshult in southern Sweden in 1707. As a boy, he reportedly learnt Latin before Swedish, which could explain why he came up with the binomial system of giving every creature and plant a double-barrelled Latin name made up of its genus and species. So, for example, brown trout are *Salmo trutta*. In his vast encyclopaedia, *Systema Naturae*, he divided life into kingdoms, then each one into phylum, then class, order, family, genus and, finally, species.

Interestingly, Linnaeus came up with the system as a sort of shorthand to help him define in his own mind groups of species. He could never have imagined how it would go on to be such a bedrock of biology. By the time of his death in 1778, he had given binomial names to about 14,000 species. Today, around 1.5 million have a Latin name.

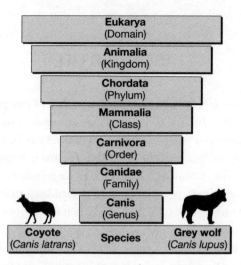

Hierarchy of biological classification

Linnaeus travelled extensively during his lifetime and was just twenty-five years old when he led the Lapland expedition. The trip was sponsored by the Royal Society of Sciences in Uppsala, where he taught at the university. While collecting specimens was a key aim of the expedition, the patrons also wanted him to gather information on the Sami – semi-nomadic people who survived by fishing, fur trapping and herding reindeer. A bit like modern-day bioprospectors studying the ways of indigenous tribes in the hope of finding cures to deadly diseases, Linnaeus had been tasked with studying how the Sami used medicinal plants. The hope was that he would bring back knowledge that could cure some of the terrible diseases of the day.

The expedition was fairly successful. Linnaeus not only acquired valuable knowledge about the Sami, such as learning about flora like the Angelica plant (a mainstay of the Sami diet that was thought to cure the plague); but he also kept a detailed journal and made many drawings of the species he encountered, as well as bringing back pressed plant specimens for later analysis.

Linnaeus was, however, slightly cheeky in moulding the truth about the extent of the journey. As he was being paid by the kilometre, he claimed the group had travelled over 7,200 kilometres and made one extra detour inland, when in fact they had covered half that distance. But that doesn't diminish his achievement at such a young age for cataloguing so much about Arctic life.

This was just the start of an incredibly successful career. Indeed, after his visit to London, in 1736, the Chelsea Physic Garden was rearranged according to his classification system. And some even claim that Charles Darwin might not have come up with his tree of life without Linnaean classification. Linnaeus's influential work is recognized on Swedish currency – his favourite flower (*Linnaea borealis*) appears on the 20-kroner note, while his face is on the 100-kroner note. He certainly deserves his place in the hearts of his countrymen and in the annals of science.

THE EXPEDITION THAT SHAPED EARTH

The sails billow in the breeze. From behind the clouds, the winter sun makes an appearance. The noisy Spanish port of Cadiz echoes in the distance. Ahead lies adventure. On board are the crew and numerous members of the French Academy of Sciences, led by astronomer Louis Godin, as well as two Spanish naval lieutenants they'd picked up in Cadiz. This French–Spanish collaboration is to be the first truly international expedition ever to be undertaken.

It was November 1735. The final destination: Quito, Peru. The aim: to end a long-running dispute between the supporters of English physicist and mathematician Isaac Newton and French mathematician René Descartes. Descartes claimed that Earth was elongated at the poles and shaped a bit like a lemon; Newton said it was flattened at the poles, like a grapefruit, because of the force exerted on it due to the rotation of the planet.

The expedition would end the dispute and change our view of the world. Yet it wasn't an overnight success – the trip lasted many years, for all sorts of reasons: sickness, fatal duels, poor planning and leadership, the complex nature of the calculations involved, and funds running out halfway through.

The problems began on the journey to Peru, when Godin fell in love with a prostitute and squandered a large sum of cash on expensive jewellery for her. That was just the start of Godin's failings. Not only was he utterly useless at taking care of the finances but he also proved to be a terrible manager, which led to bitter infighting within the group. Eventually, astronomer Pierre Bouguer took over.

The voyage to South America was the easy bit. Once there the men fought dangerous rapids, battled boggy roads and hacked their way through dense forest. By the time they made it to Quito they were exhausted and decrepit. They spent a few weeks recovering, and then started their scientific work.

The project proved to be hugely time-consuming due to its complexity and scale. The aim was to measure the length of a degree of latitude and compare it to a measurement taken back in France before the team left. From that they would be able to calculate the shape of the Earth using a combination of star sightings to determine latitude and a surveying technique known as triangulation.

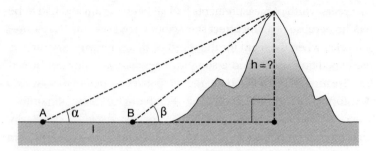

Using trigonometry, you can calculate the height (h) of a mountain
if you know the baseline length (l) and angles (α and β)

The reason they had travelled halfway around the globe to do this was that the length of a degree of latitude differs at different points on Earth because the planet's curvature is not uniform. So the further one is from the equator, the larger the distance of one degree of latitude. And taking measurements at two points that are very far apart would produce a more accurate calculation of Earth's shape.

The team started off by measuring a relatively flat stretch of land not far from Quito. After carefully surveying the terrain, using long wooden poles to build up a chain of triangles stretching for hundreds of kilometres, they then calculated the angles of the triangles using a heavy cast-iron instrument known as a quadrant, which they had to lug up and down mountains. Once they had these measurements, they took star sightings to work out the exact latitude and from that were able to accurately calculate the distance of one degree of latitude at the equator. Finally, they were able to compare the curvature of the Earth at the equator with the curvature in France, and hence work out the shape of the planet.

In total, the expedition lasted a decade. It was a long, arduous trip, beset by difficulties. At one point, one of the team realized that two years worth of measurements had all been in vain and had to be redone because of an incorrect star-sighting method. But, despite the setbacks, when the team (or those left of them) returned to Europe, the expedition was hailed a success. They had not only confirmed that Newton was right about the grapefruit-shaped Earth (which transformed naval navigation), but they had also made all sorts of other discoveries – from finding new medicinal plants previously unknown in Europe to geological breakthroughs, such as Bouguer being the first to show the effect of a mountain mass on a plumb line. (A plumb line is a weight suspended from a string, used to determine a vertical line down to the ground. Bouguer worked out that if a huge mass such as a mountain is nearby, its gravitational attraction slightly deflects the plumb line.)

Indeed, following this expedition, Europeans began to view South America in a different light – with all the cultural and scientific discoveries of the time, it's no wonder that this era became known as the Age of Enlightenment.

CABINET OF CURIOSITIES

Screaming, followed by a gunshot, echo across the sea. The crew rush to see what has caused the commotion. A 2-metre-long snake lies dead on the deck. It had escaped from the enormous jar it had been stashed in, and immediately fell victim to a terrified servant of the duchess.

The creature had been one of a collection of prize possessions of physician, collector and botanist Hans Sloane. He was returning from fifteen months in the Jamaican sunshine, where he had been working as the physician to the Duke of Albemarle – who was now lying dead in a casket on board the ship, having passed away at a fairly young age.

In 1687, the duke had been appointed Governor of Jamaica. He'd asked Sloane to accompany him and his wife to the island to work as their physician. Sloane couldn't resist the draw of adventure. What he probably hadn't accounted for was the world he was about to step foot in.

Jamaica was an English royal colony and the Duke of Albemarle had been sent to the island to help establish imperial control. This was the heyday of the transatlantic slave trade. Between 1450 and 1850, at least 12 million Africans were shipped across the ocean to colonies in the Americas and West Indies. The conditions were appalling on board – slaves were packed together and shackled in the cargo holds. It is estimated that around 20 per cent of them died on the voyage. And the fate of those that survived wasn't much better – forced to do backbreaking work on plantations across the colonies.

Sloane's main job in Jamaica was to tend to the health of the Duke of Albemarle and his retinue, but he seized the opportunity to explore this exotic island and spent any free time he had collecting hundreds of plant and animal specimens as well as writing notes on the flora, fauna and local customs.

Sloane did not appear to be concerned by the slave trade as he experienced it. He enlisted a number of slaves to help him collect specimens, and made notes in his journals about aspects of slave life and that of their masters – even noting details of the plants that were transferred from Africa to the colonies by slave traders.

His journals were also packed with information on the island's topography, weather and natural phenomena such as earthquakes, as well as detailed drawings of the exotic species he encountered and collected. Featured among his illustrations were the cocoa plant and an accompanying description of how the islanders prepared it as a medicine. Sloane found their preparation hard to digest, though, so he started mixing it with milk, which made it far more palatable.

Upon his return to the UK, he marketed 'drinking chocolate' for its medicinal value, making a small fortune from it. Many years later, two brothers by the name of Cadbury spotted its potential – and the rest is history.

Back in London, Sloane set up a medical practice but continued to add to his ever-growing collection, for which many items were imported on slave ships. His house became a veritable 'cabinet of curiosities', overflowing with stuffed creatures, plants, gems and other paraphernalia, such as a shoe made of human skin and 'ear ticklers' from China. Influential people would visit to view his collections. One such was botanist Carl Linnaeus (see page 14), whose famous work *Species Plantarum* was influenced by Sloane's notes and illustrations.

Upon Sloane's death in 1753, his wish that the vast collection of curiosities remain together was granted and the British Museum was founded to store it. It was the first public museum in the world.

So Sloane was a philanthropist, but also a man who became rich off the trappings of the slave trade – a lifestyle that all started with that expedition to Jamaica.

MONT BLANC: THE FIRST ASCENT

Brandy and courage both played their part in conquering Europe's highest mountain. Twenty-six-year-old Jacques Balmat lived with his wife in the Chamonix Valley at the foot of Mont Blanc. He earned a small wage selling crystals to collectors and hunting chamois, a species of goat-antelope. So, in 1786, when he heard about a Geneva-based scientist offering a cash prize to climb to the summit of Mont Blanc, he jumped at the chance.

Telling his wife that he was off to sell some crystals, he filled his gourd with brandy and set off to attempt to climb the formidable peak. But in those days there was no known route to the top, so this climbing challenge wasn't just physical but navigational, too.

After spending hours hunting for routes past inaccessible outcrops and deep crevasses, Balmat was eventually forced down by bad weather – although he had to spend the night on the mountain before making it safely back home.

In the eighteenth century, only those hunting chamois or crystals would risk venturing on to glaciers or climbing passes. Mountains were seen as fearsome mystical places, definitely not somewhere to be trapped on overnight. But, undeterred, Balmat tried again a few weeks later, having on the way picked up a companion – in the form of Chamonix doctor, Michel-Gabriel Paccard – and some more brandy. Maybe it was the brandy, their tenacity or sheer good fortune with the weather, but on 8 August 1786, the pair made it to the summit.

'I had reached the goal where no one had as yet been – not even the eagle nor the chamois,' Balmat later remarked.

Whether it was true that no eagle had ever landed on the top of Mont Blanc, no one knows. But what was verified was the fact that the pair reached the summit, as their progress was monitored through a telescope by a group of intrigued onlookers.

Paccard had packed a compass, a thermometer and a barometer to take measurements throughout their expedition. He also collected rock samples and noted a number of species – a butterfly, a fly and a type of bird known as a snow bunting – that had never been seen before at such high altitude.

News of the feat reached the cash-prize donor, Horace-Bénédict de Saussure (see box), a couple of days later. Paccard and Balmat claimed their reward, but tragedy awaited the latter when he returned home to find that his daughter had died the day he reached the mountaintop. A sad end to a tale of adventure and bravery. Yet the unconquerable mountain had been conquered. And with it came a new era where the sport of mountaineering was born.

The scientist sponsor

Horace-Bénédict de Saussure was born near Geneva in 1740, and made his first trip to a glacier near Chamonix at the age of twenty. In the following decades, he carried out field research all around the Alps. Always with a thermometer and barometer stashed in his backpack, he conducted all sorts of experiments on temperature and atmospheric pressure as well as electricity and magnetism. De Saussure developed the first electrometer, which measured electric charge, and an improved hygrometer to measure moisture in the atmosphere. He was the first to demonstrate the increase of solar radiation with altitude, and successfully calculated the height of Mont Blanc to within 50 metres of its known value today – 4,810 metres.

Following a failed attempt to climb to the summit of Mont Blanc, he offered a cash prize and challenged others to try. The year after Paccard and Balmat's successful ascent, the latter guided de Saussure to the top; the measurements he took there helped him to conclude that Mont Blanc was indeed the highest mountain in Europe.

THE FIRST ENVIRONMENTALIST

Crawling on hands and knees, the four men inch forward along the narrow ridge. Loose stones and snow fall over the edge, tumbling down the 300-metre drop. Their thin jackets and shoes are no match for the bitter, howling wind. Their porters had turned back at the snow line but the men, gasping in the thin air, press on towards the summit. The terrain changes to jagged rocks, ripping apart shoes, drawing blood. The weather worsens. Thunderstorms and blizzards ensue. The four never made it to the summit. The year was 1802.

At over 6,000 metres tall, Chimborazo volcano in Ecuador was at that time believed to be the highest mountain in the world (Everest didn't knock it off the top spot for another fifty years). Despite not making it to the summit, however, this was the highest that anyone had ever climbed.

Leading the expedition was German Alexander von Humboldt – a trailblazing explorer and naturalist. Humboldt used the various instruments, such as a barometer and thermometer, which he'd hauled up the mountain to take readings of the air temperature, pressure and humidity.

Indeed, his thirst for knowledge made him an exceptional scientist. This was the start of a career that saw him cement his name in the annals of science. But never has a man been so influential in life and yet so forgotten in death.

Humboldt was born in Berlin in 1769, and his aristocratic family hoped he'd run a business in mining. But he was more interested in analysing the minerals than the money. Studying natural sciences in the evening, he dreamt of travelling to distant parts of the world. His dream came true in 1799 when, along with his friend the

French naturalist Aimé Bonpland, he set sail to the New World. After a six-week voyage across the Atlantic, they landed in New Andalusia in modern-day Venezuela. This was the start of five years of exploration through Colombia, Ecuador, Peru, Mexico, Cuba and the US.

Braving blizzards on Chimborazo was just one of their many adventures. They swam in crocodile-infested waters, dodged jaguars and lived to tell their tales despite suffering symptoms of unknown yet potentially deadly diseases.

Humboldt described his thirst to explore like being perpetually chased by 'ten thousand pigs'. But not only were his observations of indigenous tribes and ancient civilizations an insight into exotic worlds; he made immense contributions to science, too. He observed everything from the rock strata below his feet to the stars above his head, revolutionizing fields from agriculture to botany, meteorology to zoology. Humboldt was a true polymath – always one to gather his own evidence. He used a microscope to study the lice on his own body and carried out experiments on electric eels, shocking himself as he dissected them with his bare hands.

But his greatest contribution is surely to the field of environmentalism. In his era, there was no such thing. At the time, humans were viewed as second only to God – sitting above the beasts and plants of the natural world – and nature was there to be exploited for the good of humankind.

On the expedition, Humboldt began to see a different picture of the world, where humans were just a spoke in the wheel of this delicately balanced planet; remove too many spokes and the wheel would spin dangerously out of control, or even stop turning altogether.

In Mexico, he noted how excessive irrigation for intensive farming had drained the local rivers and lakes. In Venezuela, he saw how the lust for pearls had wiped out oysters, and how mining had deforested vast swathes of land. Crucially, he realized that ecosystems were connected. Annihilating one species sparked a chain reaction, causing other species to decline and die out. Upsetting the delicate balance of nature would not only damage wildlife but also ultimately humans.

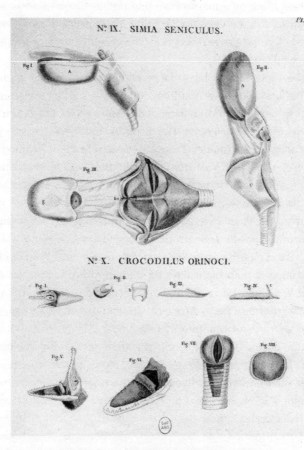

Some of Humboldt's drawings from 1801

Humboldt was also the first to recognize that the climate of an area was the product of a complex relationship between life, the land and the oceans, such as how forests are vital for keeping the planet cool, sucking up carbon dioxide. He realized plants should be classified by climate zones, not taxonomy. He came up with the idea of an isotherm – a line on a map connecting points which have the same temperature. And he even got an inkling of plate tectonics – over a century before others realized how the continents pieced together (see page 50).

At the time, Humboldt's vision of environmental degradation seemed radical. But he was still much loved – both by the scientific community and the world in general. His peers called him 'the Shakespeare of the sciences'. He inspired the likes of writer Jules Verne and scientist Charles Darwin. Indeed, Darwin claimed that Humboldt's *Personal Narrative* inspired him 'to travel in distant countries, and led me to volunteer as naturalist in Her Majesty's ship *Beagle*'. Darwin took the work with him on the *Beagle*.

At the time of his death in 1859, Humboldt was the most famous scientist in the world. Indeed, German scientist and writer Johann Wolfgang von Goethe once said that 'one learnt more from an hour in his company than eight days of studying books'. One hundred years after Humboldt died, there were celebrations of this great man's life from Europe to Africa, Australia to the US. And yet now he seems to be all but forgotten outside of academia – maybe partly due to anti-German sentiment after the First World War or possibly just due to the passage of time. Nevertheless, the name of this first environmentalist lives on in the likes of ocean currents, giant squids and asteroids – he has more things named after him than anyone else.

CROSSING THE CONTINENTAL DIVIDE

Back in the early 1800s, not much was known about what lay west beyond the Mississippi River. A few fur trappers had ventured across the water and talked of vast plains stretching for kilometres on end. President Thomas Jefferson was keen to explore those lands for political and economic gain, with the hope of increasing trade opportunities and helping to solidify an American claim on the far north-west. So he charged his personal secretary Meriwether Lewis with venturing into the unknown to try to find a route by water through to the Pacific coast.

But Jefferson wasn't just interested in the expedition for power and money; he also saw it as a chance to explore these lands and discover whether the stories of mythical beasts really were true. For years, he'd been fascinated by fossils that had been unearthed in the east – such as the remains of woolly mammoths and the so-called *Megalonyx* found in New Jersey and Virginia (which was later identified as a giant ground sloth).

When Lewis enlisted his old army friend William Clark to co-captain the expedition, he charged Clark with organizing the logistics of the trip, while Lewis would do all the scientific work, such as analysing and collecting species and fossils.

In spring 1804, Lewis, Clark and a thirty-three-man crew cast off from the banks of the Mississippi in St Louis in a 16-metre-long keelboat and two smaller wooden boats. Turning west, they headed up the Missouri. For 1,600 kilometres they slowly navigated their way along the river, at times having to resort to towing the boats from the bank or hauling them over shallow rapids.

At last, the landscape opened up into vast, flat plains – kilometre upon kilometre of endless grass. These were the lands of armies of buffalo, elk and antelope, as well as the Sioux – nomads who lived in tepees and hunted buffalo on horseback.

Lewis avidly recorded new species they encountered, such as the pronghorn antelope and prairie dog. At the time, no one knew whether woolly mammoths still existed. Lewis kept his eyes open but, of course, never spotted one – only fossils.

As the expedition ventured on west and the plains gave way to the hills of the continental divide, Lewis made more discoveries of previously unknown creatures, such as the mountain goat and the fearsome grizzly bear. Still no living woolly mammoths.

But they did encounter the Shoshone tribe, also known as the Snake Nation, who lived both east and west of the Rocky Mountains. Lewis and his corps were the first white men they had ever seen. At first nervous of these strangers from the east, the Shoshone began to realize the men weren't an immediate threat, and tentatively started sharing some food and letting them sleep in tepees.

As Lewis gazed up at the huge mountains rising in the distance, he knew that to pass over them he would need more provisions – in particular, horse power. And so began negotiations to purchase horses from the Shoshone. But they were playing hardball. It was during talks with the Shoshone chief, Cameahwait – 'One Who Never Walks' – that an incredible coincidence happened. One of Lewis's party was Sacagawea – a lady who had grown up with the Shoshones but had been kidnapped by raiding warriors from the Hidatsa tribe. Now married to a French-Canadian fur trader, Sacagawea suddenly recognized Cameahwait as her long-lost brother. After that, negotiations took a turn for the better, and Lewis was given his much-needed horses. Yet, tough times were still to come.

Some of the men returned to the keelboat and, laden with zoological and botanical treasures, they headed back to St Louis.

Guided by some of the Shoshone tribe, the rest of the men continued on west. The hills rose into steep mountains. For three months, they climbed snow-covered slopes, battled blizzards and fended off frostbite.

But, at last, the men caught a glimpse of the glistening ocean, eventually reaching the Pacific in November 1805. Lewis had hoped to hitch a lift back to civilization aboard a passing trade ship. But they had reached the coast too late. No ship sailed by. They were forced to hunker down for a miserable long winter of hunger and disease. Winter gradually turned to spring, and the snow began to melt. Eventually, the men set off, leaving the coast behind as they journeyed back over the mountains.

The return leg proved to be just as eventful as the way out. Lewis and Clark had split up to explore different areas, planning to rendezvous where the Yellowstone and Missouri rivers met. But at Marias River in modern-day Montana, Lewis and his group were attacked by warriors from the Blackfeet tribe, intent on stealing weapons and horses. Two warriors died – the only violent encounter with Native American tribes in the whole expedition. Soon afterwards, while hunting, Lewis was accidentally shot in the bottom; fortunately he survived the injury and successfully reunited with Clark.

In autumn 1806, the men limped back into St Louis, exhausted by their epic two-year journey but full of stories of incredible landscapes, intriguing people and creatures never before known to science. This was a tale of friendship, endurance and discovery. Lewis and his men never found a route by water through to the Pacific, but it was the first expedition to cross the American continental divide.

INTO THE AMAZON

'The blow-gun, in the hands of an expert adult Indian, can be made to propel arrows so as to kill at a distance of fifty and sixty yards. It is a far more useful weapon in the forest than a gun, for the report of a firearm alarms the whole flock of birds or monkeys feeding on a tree, while the silent poisoned dart brings the animals down one by one. The poison, which must be fresh to kill speedily, is obtained only of the Indians who live beyond the cataracts of the rivers flowing from the north. Its principle ingredient is the wood of the *Strychnos toxifera*.' These were the words of naturalist Henry Walter Bates, who spent eleven years in the Amazon and whose work had a big impact on Charles Darwin's theory of natural selection.

Born in Leicester in 1825, Bates was the son of a stocking-maker. While in training to take over the family business, a chance encounter changed his life for ever. In the local library he met a teacher, none other than Alfred Russel Wallace – Darwin's adversary who independently also came up with the theory of natural selection around the same time (see page 34). The pair discovered their shared love for all things creepy-crawly, and they started dreaming of travelling to foreign lands in search of new species. Four years later, they were on a ship bound for South America. Bates was just twenty-three years old, drawn by the lure of adventure in the vast rainforest he'd read about, then called the 'Amazons'.

After travelling up the Pará and Tocantins rivers, the pair parted company. Bates ventured deeper into the rainforest – his home for over a decade.

The remote depths of the Amazon were perilous. Alongside his local guides, Bates battled weather and wildlife, from extreme floods and raging currents to encounters with snakes, piranhas and alligators.

'When the net was formed into a circle, and the men had jumped in, an alligator was found to be enclosed,' Bates later recounted in his book *In the Heart of the Amazon Forest*.

First one shouted, 'I have touched his head'; then another, 'He has scratched my leg'; one of the men was thrown off his balance, and then there was no end to the laughter and shouting. At last a youth of about fourteen years of age seized the reptile by the tail, and held him tightly until, a little resistance being overcome, he was able to bring it ashore. I had cut a strong pole from a tree, and as soon as the alligator was drawn to solid ground, gave him a smart rap with it on the crown of his head, which killed him instantly. It was a good-sized individual, the jaws being considerably more than a foot long, and fully capable of snapping a man's leg in twain.

Maybe the most dangerous of all, however, was the smallest of predators – the mosquito. At various times in his travels, Bates was prey to the disease-carrying pests, contracting both yellow fever and malaria. But that didn't stop him. Once he'd recovered, he was back to punting upstream, scouring the river banks, hacking his way through dense undergrowth in search of weird and wonderful creatures. Throughout the expedition, he collected more than 14,000 specimens of birds, beasts and bugs – over half of which were new to science.

Bates' diaries and letters bring to life an intriguing world, painting a picture of the intrepid naturalist gathering and trapping different species before methodically cataloguing them as they sat in cages scattered across camp.

Mimicry

During his time in the Amazon, Bates came up with his theory of mimicry to explain the phenomenon of an organism evolving to resemble another object or organism, often to protect them from predators. Initially, he was baffled by how *Heliconius* butterflies moved so slowly yet weren't eaten by birds. Eventually, he realized it was because they were toxic, giving off a unique smell that birds knew to avoid. From this, he came up with the idea that if perfectly edible species evolved to physically resemble these butterflies, they would be protected from predation and, hence, pass on these physical traits to their offspring. Once home, Bates published his ideas about mimicry, which Charles Darwin used as a convincing argument for his theory of natural selection.

Upon his return to Britain, Bates spent three years writing up accounts of his adventures in his popular book *The Naturalist on the River Amazons*. He went on to become a well-respected scientist, because of his theory of mimicry, which he came up with during his explorations of the Amazon. So, he was not only a great explorer, but also a great naturalist and author, who through his writing brought to life his daring scientific adventures.

DARWIN'S ADVERSARY

Shouts ring out across the village: 'Tana goyang! Tana goyang! Earthquake! Earthquake!' Book in hand, naturalist and explorer Alfred Russel Wallace stays sitting in his chair as the gentle shaking grows more violent. Through the window he can see villagers streaming out of their homes, clutching frightened little ones. The house timbers creak. Had this been a European village built of bricks, homes would now be crumbling. But the timber frames stand resolutely, surviving the aftershocks that tremble all through the night and into the following week.

Wallace was in Celebes, the Indonesian island now known as Sulawesi. It was his second expedition – and a long way from the small village near Usk in Wales where he grew up.

Born in 1823, Wallace's interest in bugs, bees and other beasts developed when he was working as a teacher in Leicester in 1844, and met Henry Walter Bates, who went on to become a well-known naturalist (see page 31). Their friendship grew through their shared love of wildlife, and four years later they were on their way to the Amazon.

At first, the expedition was a huge success – the men ventured into areas never before explored by European naturalists and collected thousands of specimens, which they planned to sell later to finance their trip. But they almost didn't make it home. On the return voyage across the Atlantic, the ship caught fire and sank, dragging to the depths of Davy Jones' Locker all the collected specimens and most of the detailed field notes, save for a few drawings of plants and fish. The passengers and crew miraculously survived, picked up by a passing ship.

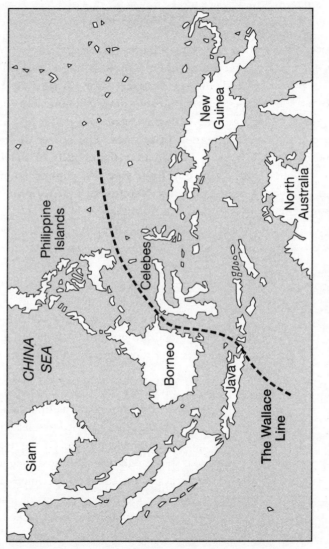

The Wallace Line marks the boundary between wildlife from the Australian region and Asia

Upon his return, Wallace tried to make the best of things. Having lost the specimens and hence his income, he wrote a book about his voyage. But, as all his detailed notes were at the bottom of the ocean, he had to rely on what he could remember – which wasn't enough to impress the scientific establishment. The book received poor reviews.

This setback didn't curtail Wallace's thirst for adventure, though. In 1853, he set sail again. This time on a voyage to the East Indies – now modern-day Indonesia and Malaysia. The earthquake he experienced on the island of Celebes was just one of the many unique adventures he had on this expedition. Covering more than 22,000 kilometres, he left Singapore in 1854 and spent eight years voyaging from Sumatra in the east to New Guinea in the west, earning his keep selling bird skins. He saw stunning Birds of Paradise in Aru, collected all sorts of beetles in Celebes, and hunted orangutans in Borneo.

But it was on this expedition that Wallace was to make potentially his greatest contribution to science. Having made the short trip across the strait between the islands of Bali and Lombok, he was walking along the beach when he realized that he could no longer hear the soft calls of Asian birds, such as woodpeckers and thrushes, but instead the raucous squawking of Australian birds like the cockatoo and the honey-eating helmeted friarbird. And yet he could see the home of the Asian birds just across the strait.

Wallace realized that the same birds would have existed on both islands once upon a time, but they had developed into different species due to the natural barrier of the strait. He speculated that this could have been caused by changes in the Earth's surface way back in geological history (although at that time no one knew about continental drift – see page 50).

Wallace deduced that creatures living either side of a geographical barrier, such as the strait or a mountain range, would gradually evolve differently. On one side of the barrier, one lot of individuals could develop a new advantageous characteristic to outcompete their neighbours that lacked the beneficial trait. Over time, individuals with this trait would reproduce, passing those characteristics on to their offspring. Hence, a new species would evolve on one side of the barrier, with the original species, which hasn't developed the new characteristic, on the other side.

It was while on the island of Gilolo (modern-day Halmahera) that Wallace posted a letter about this revolutionary idea, which was to help frame one of the most well-known theories in science – natural selection (see box).

The letter journeyed from this remote outpost in the Moluccas archipelago via Singapore, Hong Kong, Alexandria, Paris and Rotterdam, before landing in the letterbox of Down House in Bromley, Kent – the home of none other than Charles Darwin (see page 103).

In the letter, Wallace proposed his idea for how different species might evolve. Darwin too had been mulling over this idea for many years, but hadn't yet published anything on it. Wallace's letter sent Darwin into panic mode, spurring him into action. Annoyed at himself for dallying, Darwin contacted friends to ask what he should do about this scientific adversary who could end up stealing the limelight for a theory Darwin had spent years developing. The friends suggested a meeting at the Linnean Society, so that both Darwin and Wallace could present their ideas.

The meeting turned out to be a very amicable affair. Wallace was a huge fan of Darwin and held the man in such high regard that he was just pleased to have made a contribution to such a key concept in science. So, despite both naturalists having come up with the theory of natural selection independently, it is Darwin who will forever be remembered for it in the annals of science because of his famous book *On the Origin of Species*. Wallace never begrudged him for it. Indeed, Wallace went on to have a very successful career – in his own mind helped by his association with Darwin. And he made many other great contributions to science, such as his 1904 book *Man's Place in the Universe*, which was the first by a biologist to discuss whether life might exist on other planets, including Mars. Wallace was a scientist not intent on fame, but simply hungry to understand the world around him.

Natural selection

Natural selection is the flame that fuels evolution. It's a process whereby some organisms within a species develop beneficial physical or behavioural traits that enable them to survive better in their environment than individuals from the same species that lack those useful traits. These beneficial traits become more common in the population because more of the offspring with the useful traits survive.

This concept is often called 'survival of the fittest'. But this is slightly misleading. Firstly, being 'fit' isn't about being stronger, it's about being able to survive better in that particular environment and hence be able to reproduce. Secondly, the environmental pressures (such as competition for food or mates) that force nature to choose between organisms of the same species sift out the worst of the bunch rather than picking out the best. So, rather than 'survival of the fittest' it might be more apt to say 'elimination of the least fit'. Darwin didn't understand the mechanism of how trait changes happened, as he knew nothing about genetics. It wasn't until the early 1900s that scientists understood the mechanism of genetics, and how it is mutations in genes that cause trait changes.

PASTEUR DEVELOPS PASTEURIZATION

Ice and snow crunch under foot. Microbiologist and chemist Louis Pasteur is careful of where to tread for fear of slipping on the path. With the smell of pine trees in his nostrils, his mule takes him up the mountainside. The air thins. Rounding another bend, the trees give way to an incredible vista – a vast field of ice that stretches all the way up the valley. The Mer de Glace. He carefully unloads the glass flasks. There are twenty flasks in total, each filled with a liquid. One by one, he removes the flask's stoppers and briefly exposes the contents to the air.

Pasteur's theory was that at this high altitude of around 2,000 metres the air would be relatively germ free compared to at lower altitudes, which would probably contain more microbes. Prior to the climb, he had boiled the liquid in all of the flasks bar one. By comparing the contents of these flasks with fifty others (which he'd also pre-heated, exposing twenty of them to air at sea level and twenty to air at 850 metres), Pasteur was testing his theory that pre-heating a liquid kills any microbes within it.

He was proven right. Microbes developed in eight of the twenty flasks exposed to air at sea level, yet in only five in the flasks exposed at an altitude of 850 metres. And just one of the flasks exposed to the air on the Mer de Glace was contaminated with microbes. Pasteur's experiments in the early 1860s confirmed his germ theory.

However, at first it met with resistance. For thousands of years, society had believed that living organisms could develop from non-living matter – fleas from dust or maggots from dead flesh. Pasteur's germ theory finally put an end to these ideas and revolutionized our understanding of healthcare by showing that many diseases are caused by microbes.

Off the back of this breakthrough with germ theory, Napoleon III approached Pasteur with a problem that was facing France's wine industry.

Wine was spoiling while in transit. Pasteur clocked that this must be because it was being contaminated. But boiling the wine wasn't an option because that would ruin the taste. So Pasteur experimented with what temperature was sufficient to kill off microbes. He found that 55 degrees Celsius seemed to do the trick, yet didn't spoil the wine.

The heat-treating process became known as pasteurization. Today, most milk is pasteurized to remove any harmful bacteria. Indeed, before the 1922 Milk and Dairies Act, thousands had died from bovine tuberculosis – a fatal microbe sometimes found in unpasteurized milk.

So, Pasteur saved not only the French wine industry but also thousands of lives. Yet there was more to come. He also rescued the failing French silk industry after his studies revealed that a silkworm infection was being transmitted by parasites, and suggested the infected worms should be removed and destroyed.

Finally, Pasteur came up with a way of creating vaccines. After injecting an old culture of bacteria into his chickens, the birds became ill but didn't die – and were then immune to cholera. Pasteur quickly realized that he could expose animals to weaker strains of a disease to build up their immunity. A century before, Dr Edward Jenner had discovered that cowpox protected against smallpox (see box), but Pasteur was the first to create vaccines in the lab.

Pasteur went on to develop vaccines for other diseases, such as anthrax and rabies. Indeed, few people can be credited with saving more lives than this great microbiologist, whose early work on germ theory on the slopes of Mont Blanc set him up for a lifetime of discovery.

> **Fighting the pox**
>
> In 1796, Dr Edward Jenner acted on a hunch that milkmaids who suffered the mild disease of cowpox never contracted smallpox. He'd watched how the perfect complexion of milkmaid Sarah Nelmes remained unblemished, despite her coming into contact with cows suffering from the pox. Intrigued, he decided to test his theory that a small dose of cowpox ensured protection from smallpox. He injected pus from a cowpox blister into the arm of eight-year-old James Phipps. The child became immune.
>
> Despite the idea being widely ridiculed, Jenner submitted a paper to the Royal Society, who asked for more proof. Undaunted, he inoculated a number of children, including his own eleven-month-old son. Jenner coined the word 'vaccine' from the Latin for cow – 'vacca'. The disease was eventually eradicated in the twentieth century through a concerted global vaccination programme. The last natural case of smallpox was in Somalia in 1977, although in 1978 someone contracted the disease following an accident in a lab in Birmingham.

THE ADVENTURESS ARTIST

Marianne North watches as the beetle slowly climbs up the ladder-like structure on the outside of the pitcher plant, lured by the sweet nectar under the lip at the top. Feasting on the nectar, it loses its balance, slipping through the 'mouth' of the plant into a pool of digestive enzymes. Writhing around in the liquid, the helpless creature faces a slow, hideous death.

Paintbrush in hand, paper at the ready, North is perched halfway up a hill in the Malaysian state of Sarawak in Borneo. Squeezing oil on to the wooden palette, she dabs a little on the brush then starts to paint, filling in her rough sketch of the pitcher plant and surrounding lush vegetation.

Most botanical pictures of that time were painted in watercolour, while traditional scientific illustrations were simply detailed anatomical drawings. But North blurred the line between science and art by working in oil – still managing to capture fine details, yet bringing the plants to life with vivid colours.

Indeed, North was never one to follow the crowd. Not only as an artist but also as a naturalist. Unlike most naturalists of her day, who shot, captured or dug up species and took them home, North just relied on her paintings to capture the essence of the creatures and plants she encountered. Plus, she was a lone female explorer in an era when women rarely travelled solo, let alone abroad to exotic and sometimes dangerous locations around the world.

North was born in 1830 in the south-coast town of Hastings. Her father was the MP for Hastings and the family were wealthy landowners. After her mother died, she began painting plants, her interest possibly spurred on by her father's friendship with the director at Kew Gardens. Then, when her father lost his seat in parliament, the pair started travelling together, visiting Europe, the Middle East and North Africa. When her father died, North was devastated, hiding from her grief by immersing herself in her paintings.

But before long, faraway lands were beckoning once more. With no husband tying her down – 'Marriage? A terrible experiment' – and plenty of money at her disposal, North was free to explore the world to her heart's content. So, with various 'letters of introduction' in her luggage, in 1871, at the age of forty, she set sail across the Atlantic.

In those days, letters of introduction were like social networks today, allowing the upper classes to connect with one another all around the British Empire. Charles Darwin even wrote one of these letters of introduction for North. And, unlike ladies back home, who were so often exempt from academia, these connections meant that she was privy to meeting great intellectuals and influential people, from ambassadors to viceroys to rajahs, all over the world. She dined with the President of the United States and stayed with the Rajah and Rani of Sarawak. But conventional society bored her. It was exploration and discovery in remote places that really piqued her interest.

In the US, North marvelled at the giant redwoods and Niagara Falls; in Brazil she hacked her way through the Amazon; in India she rode an elephant; in Japan she drank tea in quaint teahouses; in Australia she cosied up to koalas. She described her life as a chance to 'wander and wonder and paint!'

Exploration in those days was not easy. Many deemed travel an unsuitable pursuit for the 'weaker sex'. For anyone, ocean voyages were long and living conditions basic. Overland trekking to remote locations was no less arduous and often dangerous. But North relished the challenge, travelling light with just a few items of clothing and her precious oils and brushes stuffed into a single small suitcase.

In 1881, she took a year off from travel, returning to Britain to prepare an exhibition of her paintings in a gallery at Kew Gardens that was built specifically for her work and paid for out of her own pocket. With photographs still only in black and white, her vivid paintings of wildlife and the landscapes surrounding them fascinated the public, giving them a glimpse into these exotic worlds. A gallery of her paintings still exists there today.

North was truly a Victorian trailblazer, whose adventurous spirit helped document hundreds of plant species from far-flung lands, many of which were new to science. Indeed, one genus and four plant species are named after her. She was a talented artist, intrepid explorer and respected naturalist, and very much mistress of her own destiny.

THE FATHER OF MODERN POLAR EXPLORATION

The first rowing boat splashes into the roiling ocean. Then a second is lowered into the waves. One by one the six men shake hands with the captain of the sealing ship and climb down the ladder. As they cast off, the ship fires a cannon salute goodbye before turning back towards the vast ocean and eventually disappearing on the horizon. Oars cutting through choppy waters, the boats begin to hunt for a route through the icebergs. But land is elusive.

For almost two weeks they battled strong currents. Eventually, exhausted, they landed on an island, but it took another two weeks to finally make it to the mainland – the vast wilderness of Greenland.

Previous attempts to cross Greenland had ended in failure. But leading this intrepid team of six was Norwegian Fridtjof Nansen. He believed others had failed because they had started on the inhabited west coast, where there was always civilization to run back to when things got tough. So, by landing on the unpopulated east coast, there was no going back.

It's not many winners of the Nobel Peace Prize that have undertaken an expedition like this. But Fridtjof Nansen was no ordinary man. A zoologist, explorer, diplomat, writer, artist and humanitarian, he spoke at least five languages, produced maps and stunning illustrations of species from his travels, he helped repatriate prisoners of war after the First World War, earning him the prize in 1922.

And, crucially for science, he came up with a few groundbreaking theories, from the nature of the central nervous system to the idea that an ocean current carried Arctic polar ice from east to west. Indeed, not many people are as adept with a microscope as with an ice axe. He was no jack of all trades, but master of many.

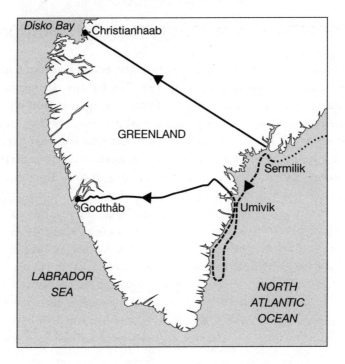

Nansen's planned route was from Sermilik to Christianhaab,
but his actual route took him to Godthåb

Born in 1861 in the town Store Froen, near Oslo, his lawyer
father was a devoutly religious man and instilled in young Fridtjof a
sense of humanitarianism. Meanwhile, his mother encouraged him
and his siblings to explore the outdoors. Fridtjof grew into a talented
skater and swimmer – but also an expert skier. This skill set him
up for a life of adventure. The intrepid young man could cover 80
kilometres on skis, with just his dog for company.

Nansen had been on many an adventure before, but none was

quite like the one he undertook in 1888. It took his team two months to cross the frozen wasteland of Greenland. They survived extreme hardship, battling vicious storms and bitter temperatures of −45 degrees Celsius, and climbed a mountain dome 2,700 metres above sea level.

But the expedition wasn't just about getting from A to B. The scientist inside Nansen was hard at work. During those arduous days, he pondered on the nature and causes of ice ages, and gained invaluable insight into the conditions in northern Europe during the last glacial period.

The trip was also instrumental in modernizing the equipment used for polar exploration. He pioneered the concept of layering clothing for extra warmth, as opposed to wearing huge thick furs.

The world's hardiest ship

On a hunch, in 1893, Nansen let his ship be frozen into drifting pack ice off the Siberian coast. Many saw this voyage as pure lunacy. But, ever determined, Nansen wanted to prove his theory that a current carried polar ice from east to west. So, he built a wooden schooner with a reinforced hull, which proved to be an engineering marvel. The *Fram* survived three years of crushing pressure from the Arctic ice. And, true to Nansen's theory, it popped out of the ice on 13 August 1896 near Spitsbergen – an archipelago between mainland Norway and the North Pole.

Nansen wasn't on board. He had realized the ship wasn't going to pass over the North Pole and so, leaving most of the crew on the vessel, he and one companion (as well as 28 dogs and 100 days' rations) struck out on sledge. He never made it to the North Pole, but he did get closer than anyone had ever done before.

On its three-year voyage, the *Fram* gathered six volumes worth of observations, revolutionizing polar science and gaining Nansen a professorship of oceanography in 1908.

Ever resourceful, Nansen also came up with a way of covering a lot of ground in a short space of time. By fashioning his tent into a sail, he used the strong winds to 'ski sail' across many kilometres. And, when the team finally made it to the west coast but civilization still lay 80 kilometres away over a mountain range, he chose not to climb it and instead built a boat from local wood and rowed the last leg to the town of Godthåb.

Nansen is rightly known as the father of modern polar exploration. Indeed, his ideas influenced many future expeditions.

THE PETTICOAT-WEARING EXPLORER

Mary Henrietta Kingsley perches precariously in the game pit, the thick layers of her skirt the only thing protecting her legs from the 30-centimetre-long spikes at the bottom of the trap. She feels relieved she's not opted for trousers – the lack of material would have been her demise. Instead, she is wearing her usual outfit – a long, layered skirt, high-necked blouse and boots. Except for the colourful flowers adorning her hair, pulled back off her face, she wouldn't have looked out of place on a street in London. But this is no urban landscape. This is a rainforest near the West African village of Efoua. One of the many exotic lands on the continent, which Kingsley explored during her all-too-brief years of travel.

Kingsley was born in Islington, London, in 1862. She was the daughter of the doctor, traveller and writer George Kingsley and his wife, Mary. While her father lived an exciting life, tending to aristocratic patients or joining expeditions to the likes of America, China and India, Mary (junior) had to contend with being an armchair traveller – exploring her father's vast library filled with volumes on science and exploration. And, while her brother was able to go to Cambridge University, Mary never received an education – she didn't even go to school.

At the age of twenty-six, Kingsley made her first trip abroad – although that was just a quick visit to Paris. It wasn't until her parents died in short succession when she was thirty that she was able to spread her wings and explore the world. She headed to Africa, hungry for adventure and the chance to pursue her anthropological interests and collect specimens of foreign creatures.

Kingsley's detailed drawings of some of the fish she encountered on her travels

At that time, the few women who ventured to Africa went as the wives of administrators or missionaries. Kingsley travelled solo. Stepping off the boat in Freetown, Sierra Leone, she had rum, gin, tobacco and cloth stashed away in her bags, ready to barter for ivory and rubber. But it wasn't long before she was heading into the wild – the first of many adventures.

Kingsley's encounters with wildlife were often eventful, like when she had to prod a hippo with her umbrella or fend off a croc with a paddle. As she later recalled in her book, *The Congo and the Cameroons*, these encounters were often a little too close to be comfortable: 'On one occasion, a mighty Silurian, as the *Daily Telegraph* would call him, chose to get his front paws over the stern of my canoe, and endeavoured to improve our acquaintance. I had to retire to the bows, to keep the balance right, and fetch him a clip on the snout with a paddle.'

Kingsley not only kept a note of all her adventures but also collected specimens of previously unknown species of fish, snakes and insects, which she gave to the British Museum in London.

Sadly, her adventures were cut short when she contracted typhoid fever while helping out as a volunteer nurse in the Boer War in South Africa. She died on 3 June 1900, before being buried at sea (eventually – the coffin refused to sink and so a spare anchor had to be used to weigh it down).

In the brief years that she travelled, Kingsley explored remote parts of Africa, came face to face with its most fearsome creatures, became the first woman to climb Mount Cameroon (the highest peak in West Africa), and wrote two books – one of which was a bestseller and is still in print. Her down-to-earth attitude made her hugely popular with indigenous people, as did her critical attitude to colonialism. Meanwhile, her humorous tone in her books and ability to play down the hardships of life in the African wilderness brought her huge respect back home. And she was not only a great explorer, but also a great naturalist – with three species of fish named after her.

THE MAN WHO MOVED EARTH

A penknife has already claimed the frostbitten toes of one of the group – Fritz Loewe. Temperatures of –60 degrees Celsius, hunger and extreme fatigue are conspiring against Alfred Wegener and his team. And the route markers back to civilization that they had so carefully laid on their outward journey are now buried under the deep, fresh snow. Desperate, Wegener and another teammate, Rasmus Villumsen, split from the others, striding on towards the next camp. But they are never to be seen alive again.

Wegener dropped dead, probably from a heart attack. After burying his body and marking the grave with skis, Villumsen ventured on. But he never made it to the camp. Wegener's body was later found but Villumsen's never was.

This expedition to Greenland in 1930 was the sad finale to a life of exploration, as Wegener strove to prove his then-radical theory of continental drift. The irony is that his body now lies about a couple of metres further from his home in Germany than when it was buried, due to continental drift.

Born in 1880, Wegener gained a PhD in astronomy from the University of Berlin and then moved into the burgeoning fields of climatology and meteorology. He developed the idea of using balloons to track air circulation, which he studied on an expedition to Greenland in 1906.

A photograph from Wegener's fourth and last expedition in 1930

On his return, he became a tutor at the University of Marburg. It was while there that he came across a paper in the library describing identical plants and animals on opposite sides of the Atlantic. Intrigued, he looked for more examples of similar-looking flora and fauna separated by oceans.

The theory at the time was that bridges of land once connected continents, but were now sunken below the waves. Wegener, however, didn't buy this idea. Through his research, he noticed that the Karoo rock strata in South Africa were identical to Santa Catarina strata in Brazil, while fern fossils from tropical climes matched those found on Spitsbergen in the Arctic. Wegener started to wonder whether these places were once connected, with creatures and seeds roaming free across one enormous continental mass. The only way this could be was if the continents moved.

In 1912, he gave a lecture at the Greenough Club – the undergraduate geological society at University College London – to explain his idea of continental drift. His subsequent work *The Origin of Continents and Oceans*, published in 1915, described how there had once been a huge single landmass, which he called Urkontinent – 'primal continent' (see box). Over time, this supercontinent was torn apart and the pieces drifted away from one another to form the continents seen today.

This concept wasn't completely new. Way back in 1596, Flemish geographer and cartographer Abraham Ortelius came up with the radical idea that the land beneath his feet was moving. On his travels around the world, making maps for the likes of the King of Spain, Philip II, he noticed that the coastlines of South America and Africa seemed to fit together like a jigsaw puzzle. Then, in 1889, Italian geologist Roberto Mantovani suggested that there might once have been one vast supercontinent. It was Wegener, though, who first revealed physical evidence of continental drift. But what Wegener didn't know was exactly how the continents moved.

If you stripped away the oceans and viewed Earth from space, it would look a bit like a football with different-sized panels stitched together. Except the panels all shift around. These so-called 'tectonic plates' float on a fluid layer called the 'asthenosphere', which is driven by hot, convective currents deep within the mantle.

Tectonic plates collide at what is known as a 'subduction zone'. As oceanic crust tends to be denser than continental crust, it is forced down beneath the other, melting at depth before rising up to the surface as magma and firing out of volcanoes as lava.

Where plates of continental crust collide, there is usually no subduction and the crust simply crumples, forcing the land upwards, as is the case with the Himalayas.

If the two plates are moving away from one another, the crust rips apart and melted mantle rock from the asthenosphere below

Pangea

Permian 250 million years ago

Laurasia

Gondwanaland

Triassic 200 million years ago

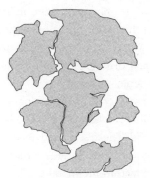

Jurassic 145 million years ago

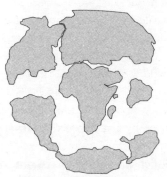

Cretaceous 66 million years ago

Over millennia, continental drift has torn apart the original
supercontinent, Pangea

flows out, filling the gap in a process known as 'seafloor spreading',
which happens at mid-ocean ridges.

At first, Wegener's theory was deemed to be pseudo-science.

It wasn't until the 1960s when evidence was found for seafloor spreading (see page 131) that Wegener's theory of continental drift became mainstream. Sadly, of course, he didn't live to see that day.

Supercontinent

Tectonic plates can move up to 10 centimetres a year (as fast as your fingernails would grow, if you didn't cut them). It may not sound like much but, over the course of millennia, the continents have shifted thousands of kilometres.

Around 250 million years ago, the continents formed one supercontinent – Wegener's Urkontinent – which we now know as Pangea, meaning 'all the Earth' in Greek.

Gradually, continental drift tore the pieces of land apart. Around 200 million years ago, Pangea divided into two – Laurasia (which was made up of modern-day Europe, Asia and North America) and Gondwanaland (which consisted of Antarctica, Australia, Africa and South America). In 250 million years' time, experts predict that another supercontinent will form, which they're calling Pangea Proxima.

DISCOVERING COSMIC RAYS

The flame roars overhead as the pilot pulls down on the lever. The balloon rises higher. Victor Hess spies a horse-drawn carriage, now the size of a child's toy. The basket creaks. Higher and higher they rise. Hess can feel his heart thumping. He glances at the altimeter. Never before have they been so high: 3,500 metres; 4,000 metres; 5,000; 5,200; 5,300 … Signalling to the pilot, Hess pulls out his electroscope in order to measure the atmospheric radiation.

It was the morning of 7 August 1912. At the time, the prevailing theory was that such radiation came from rocks on Earth. Hess wasn't convinced. In order to disprove that theory, over the course of about five months, he had made six balloon flights – both in the day and at night – bravely soaring to ever greater heights.

His measurements taken during these flights showed that the radiation varied with altitude – at 500 metres it was less than on the ground, but above 1,800 metres it started to rise, increasing substantially above 4,000 metres. At 5,300 metres it was almost three times that at sea level. This could only mean one thing: the radiation didn't come from Earth, but from space.

Hess had already ruled out the sun as the source, since he intentionally coincided one of the balloon flights with a near-total solar eclipse. As the radiation didn't dip during the eclipse, he believed it couldn't be coming from the sun, but instead had to be from outer space. Hess had discovered what were to become known as 'cosmic rays' (see box on page 56).

Victor Hess was born on 24 June 1883 in Waldstein Castle, Austria, the son of a forester to a prince. But a life of chopping down trees wasn't for him. After graduating from Graz University in 1905, he went on to do a doctorate before working at the Physical Institute in Vienna, where Professor von Schweidler inspired him with the recent discoveries in radioactivity. But it was while working as an assistant at the Institute of Radium Research of the Viennese Academy of Sciences that he came up with the idea for the hot-air balloon flights to try to ascertain the source of atmospheric radiation.

The results from the seven flights were to open a new window into astronomy and the universe. As the balloon touched down in a field near the German town of Pieskow on that morning of 7 August, Hess knew he'd discovered something important. A farmer offered to take the men in a horse-drawn carriage to the train station. From there they headed to Berlin, then home to Vienna.

Hess rushed to publish his results in the *Proceedings of the Viennese Academy of Sciences*, writing: 'The first results of my observations are most easily explained by the assumption that radiation of very high penetrating power enters the atmosphere from above and creates, even in the lowest layers, a part of the ionization observed in closed vessels.'

But it wasn't until 1926 when Robert Millikan confirmed Hess's theory, and coined the term 'cosmic ray'. Hess was subsequently awarded the Nobel Prize in Physics in 1936.

What are cosmic rays?

Travelling at blistering speeds from outer space, high-energy particles smash into Earth's atmosphere, fragmenting into smaller subatomic particles, such as pions and muons. Cosmic rays are all around us, passing through our bodies all the time – around one muon per second travels through the volume equivalent to someone's head. No one really knows exactly where cosmic rays come from. Some scientists think it could be from explosions of distant stars.

THE WORST JOURNEY IN THE WORLD

In a brown case in a drawer in a back room at the Natural History Museum are three eggs. Each one is the size of a mango and milky white in colour. These are emperor penguin eggs. The story of how they made it from the frozen wastelands of Antarctica to London is relatively unknown. But the men who retrieved the eggs from a remote penguin colony were part of one of the most infamous expeditions of all time.

The *Terra Nova*, a Dundee-built whaler, set sail from Cardiff on 15 June 1910. At its helm was Captain Robert Falcon Scott. His mission: to be the first to reach the South Pole – the most remote place on Earth.

Scott had already set foot on the continent. Between 1901 and 1904, alongside Dr Edward Wilson and a young Ernest Shackleton, he had made it to just 660 kilometres from the pole before making the wise decision to head for home.

A few years later and he was on course for Antarctica once more. But he wasn't the only one. Norwegian Captain Roald Amundsen was a well-known explorer in his own right, and also keen to be the first to the South Pole. But while Scott talked publicly about his planned attempt, Amundsen kept quiet – only revealing his intentions in a telegram when Scott stopped in Australia: 'Beg leave to inform you *Fram* proceeding Antarctic. Amundsen'.

This telegram signalled the start of one of the greatest races of all time. A race that pitted not only man against man but also man against the elements. Scott famously lost the race, reaching the pole on 17 January 1912, thirty-three days after Amundsen. He found the Norwegian flag already flying, and a tent of supplies and a note for Scott to deliver to the King of Norway in case he didn't make it back home.

But it was Scott and his team who never returned. Ravaged by starvation, hypothermia and scurvy, the five men struggled back towards the camp. On 17 March, recognizing that he was holding back the others, Captain Oates walked out of the tent, famously saying: 'I'm just going outside and may be some time …' A few days later the rest of the men succumbed to the cold, marooned in their tents by a blizzard.

But in the winter before this tragic event, many of Scott's team had been busy carrying out numerous scientific objectives. One such was to try to prove the link between birds and reptiles. At the time, ornithologists believed (incorrectly) that emperor penguins were a primitive type of bird, and that the stages of a developing foetus reflected the evolution of that species. So studying the development of an emperor penguin in the egg would reveal the missing evolutionary link between dinosaurs and birds – maybe one with some reptilian-like scales. The only way to find out was to collect eggs from a colony in Antarctica and take them back to civilization for research.

But emperor penguins breed only in the middle of the Antarctic winter (the northern hemisphere summer). So this meant trekking to the colony at a time of year when the sun never rose and the weather was at its most extreme.

On 27 June 1911, three of Scott's team, Edward Wilson, Henry Bowers and Apsley Cherry-Garrard set off from the base at Cape Evans, aiming for a known penguin colony at Cape Crozier over 100 kilometres away. For six weeks they battled the elements – navigating by candlelight and the stars, coping with temperatures that plunged to −60 degrees Celsius.

The men endured great hardships. Wilson lost an eye to a stray bit of boiling blubber from a camp stove. Frostbite nibbled at their toes. At one point their tent blew away in a blizzard and for two days they huddled in their sleeping bags, exposed to the elements, until eventually the winds subsided and they found the tent again. For sections of the trip, the snow was so thick that all three of them had to pull one sled and return for the other. This meant that for every kilometre they moved forward they actually covered three.

Eventually, the men reached the colony, with the penguins huddled together at the foot of a cliff face. Navigating their way down the cliff in the pitch black was to prove one of the most challenging moments of the expedition – but the men managed it and obtained

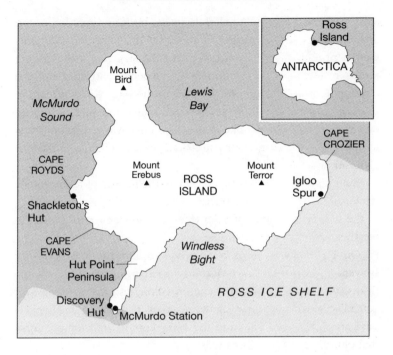

five eggs. Sadly, on the return journey, Cherry-Garrard slipped and broke two of them. The other three made it back, protected inside the men's mittens.

On 1 August, they staggered back into the base – wretched sights to behold. Their frozen clothes had to be cut off them. Cherry-Garrard was in the worst state – and hence he didn't join Scott's party that later made the push for the South Pole. This was to save his life. Scott and the men never returned. Their bodies were later found by a search party.

Shocked by these events, Cherry-Garrard felt a huge responsibility to ensure that the emperor penguin eggs made it safely back to London. Back at the Natural History Museum, two of the three embryos were cut into thin sections and mounted on to slides. Science later proved that emperor penguins weren't a useful link between birds and reptiles after all. But Cherry-Garrard did immortalize the egg expedition in his book *The Worst Journey in the World*, and it was a good example of the lengths that explorers go to in order to answer scientific questions. Indeed, all of the expedition's scientific work helped to lay the foundations of Antarctic science.

PROVING EINSTEIN RIGHT

Liverpool, 7 March 1919. Crate after crate is being loaded on to a steamship. As one after the other thumps on to deck, four men watch nervously from the dock, hopeful that the precious telescope equipment packed carefully inside each of the crates won't get broken. After all, this is just the start of a long voyage – ahead lie many potentially hazardous days at sea.

The next day, the steamship sets sail to the island of Madeira. On board are astronomers Arthur Eddington, Andrew Crommelin and Charles Davidson, as well as clockmaker Edwin Cottingham. But on arrival in Madeira, the group parts company. Crommelin and Davidson stay on the *Anselm*, heading west across the Atlantic, bound for the Brazilian city of Sobral. Eddington and Cottingham voyage south aboard the SS *Portugal* to the island of Principe, off the West African coast.

But both expeditions have the same goal: to prove one of the most fundamental theories in physics today. A theory that was to turn a relatively unknown yet talented physicist into a scientific legend.

In 1915, Albert Einstein published a paper introducing his theory of general relativity. Einstein claimed that space and time are combined in a universal fabric – spacetime – the structure of which can be warped, bent and twisted by massive objects in motion. At the time, Einstein's theory drew criticism from some scientists, as it contradicted the established view of Newtonian physics, which explains how forces act on objects. But others were intrigued by the idea and decided to try to observe this warping of spacetime in action.

The sun is the most massive object in the solar system. According to Einstein's theory, light from background stars that graze the sun should be bent ever so slightly. But, as the sun is so bright, the only way to test this phenomenon is during a solar eclipse, when the moon passes directly in front of the sun, covering its disc and revealing the surrounding stars.

Scientists from the Royal Society and Royal Astronomical Society realized that the best chance to view such a total solar eclipse would be on 29 May 1919. With time on their hands, they started investigating the best locations from which to observe it, narrowing it down to Sobral and Principe – where, they hoped, cloudless skies would provide ideal conditions for observing the sun crossing the bright Hyades star cluster.

In January and February 1919, Eddington measured the actual positions of the stars (see box). Then he started preparing for the expedition to Principe, so that when his team eventually landed on the island in April 1919 they had time to hunt around for the best spot to observe the eclipse. They settled on a cocoa plantation, as far as possible from the mountains that might attract clouds, which would run the risk of obscuring the eclipse. Lugging all the kit to this remote plantation was something of a challenge – a tram took it part of the way, but it then had to be carried for the last kilometre. The team made it with plenty of time to

How light 'bends'

According to Einstein's theory of general relativity, gravity bends the path of light. So during an eclipse the light rays from stars that graze the edge of the sun should appear ever so slightly deflected from their actual position. This is now known as gravitational lensing and has become a key tool in astrophysics for studying stars and galaxies tucked behind huge objects.

spare, spending the next few weeks setting up and testing all the equipment.

But, in the days leading up to the eclipse, stormy weather blew in. And on the morning of the 29th a heavy thunderstorm threatened to ruin the whole expedition. The eclipse was due just after 2 p.m. All the men could do was sit and wait – and hope. As noon came and went, the storm began to pass. Yet still clouds hovered overhead. But, at last, very gradually they started to break up – until patches of clear sky signalled the trip might not be in vain. They were in luck.

The eclipse lasted six minutes and fifty-one seconds. It was actually one of the longest that century and gave just enough time to capture some images of the Hyades star cluster.

The plan had been to analyse the results there and then. But, with rumour of an impending strike at the steamship company, the men hopped on the first boat home to ensure they wouldn't be marooned on the island for the next few months. And, so, after swinging by Lisbon on the return voyage, they landed back in Liverpool on 14 July.

The expedition was heralded a success – and absolved Eddington from the threat of jail. Before going on the trip, as a Quaker he had refused to sign up to military service, which warranted time behind bars. Astronomer Royal Frank Dyson had stepped in and convinced the powers that be that Eddington's duty to his country would be fulfilled by going on this expedition. Indeed it was.

After analysing the observations from both Principe and Sobral, Eddington was able to prove that predictions made by the theory of general relativity were correct, propelling Einstein into the limelight and cementing his place in scientific history.

THE AMOROUS BUTTERFLY COLLECTOR

Lying face down on the side of the path, net in hand, a thought flashes through Margaret Fountaine's mind. Most ladies in their seventies would be like the grandmothers she saw in the upmarket hotel she is staying at in Trinidad – fussing over grandchildren, dressing up for dinner. Not covered in dirt, lying stock still, hoping to trap another butterfly. How different her life could have been if she'd settled down with one of the many suitors she'd had throughout her life.

Born in Norwich in 1862, Fountaine was the eldest of seven children of clergyman John Fountaine and his wife Mary Isabella. Fountaine's love of butterflies developed as a young girl, but it wasn't until she was in her late twenties that she became financially independent – courtesy of a wealthy uncle – and was able to spread her own wings and set off on adventures abroad. To begin with, she travelled to Europe with her sisters, but before long she wanted to explore further afield on her own.

Without a passport or many specific dates recorded in her diaries, however, it's hard to pinpoint exactly where she travelled and when. Although it is possible to track down a few clues. Papers published in the journal *The Entomologist* give an idea of when she visited different countries in the Middle East. What we do know is that over the course of many decades on the road she travelled through six of the seven continents, often exploring remote regions with a guide or translator.

One guide in particular became her long-term travel companion – and lover. She met Khalil Neimy in Damascus. She was thirty-nine, he was twenty-four. Together they travelled through Algeria, Spain, Corsica, Yugoslavia, Rhodesia, Mozambique, Ceylon, Tibet and Australia. They'd gone to Australia so that Neimy could become a British citizen, which would make it easier for them to get married. But, reputedly, a dream he had intervened and the couple parted ways – for a while at least, as they met up again numerous times over the next twenty-five years.

After the first break-up, Fountaine ventured on alone, her obsession with capturing and cataloguing butterflies spurring her on adventures around the globe. Her work informed scientific knowledge and blurred the boundaries between amateurs and professionals, while also challenging gender stereotypes of the time.

In 1912, she was invited to a meeting with the Linnean Society – a club dedicated to the study of natural history but that was traditionally open only to men. This invite was revolutionary, bearing in mind that just fifteen years previously the author and naturalist Beatrix Potter wasn't allowed to attend a Linnean Society reading of her own paper because she was a woman. Yet, still, Fountaine is recognized in the annals of history as simply an avid collector of butterflies rather than as a lepidopterist.

Fountaine died in Trinidad on 21 April 1940. She was seventy-seven. She had been exploring along a path on Mount St Benedict when she suffered a heart attack. The Benedictine monk who discovered her, Brother Bruno, reportedly found her clutching a butterfly net in one hand. Rather fitting for this butterfly-obsessed adventurer.

Fountaine was buried in an unmarked grave at Woodbrook Cemetery in Port of Spain. Upon her death, she had asked for her butterfly collection to be donated to Norwich Castle Museum – along with a tin box. As instructed by her, the box wasn't to be opened for another few decades. But when it was, the twelve large volumes of diaries inside gave an intriguing insight into her life. They included intricate sketches of larvae and pupae (which are now kept in the Natural History Museum in London) and detailed notes from her travels, revealing not only the work of a great lepidopterist but also a window into her heart and her many romantic liaisons.

The then assistant editor of the *Sunday Times* edited excerpts from the diaries into a book, *Love Among the Butterflies*, which made Fountaine almost as famous for her numerous amorous endeavours as she was for being a talented naturalist. During her lifetime, she captured and catalogued over 20,000 species of butterfly, collected in sixty countries on six continents over fifty years. Fountaine was a revolutionary who loved men, loved nature and, above all, loved adventure.

CROSSING THE DARIÉN GAP

Visibility is no more than 20 metres. Walls of thick vegetation rise up on all sides. Above lies a canopy of branches and leaves, creating an umbrella that blocks out the sun. The constant drip, drip, drip a reminder of the extreme humidity. The oppressive atmosphere intensified by the sounds of the rainforest – the hum of harassing mosquitoes, chattering birds, the odd screaming monkey, croaking frogs, whose chorus intensifies as dusk falls, growing into a deafening crescendo. Fireflies emerge.

Exhausted, the team stops to set up camp for the night. Hanging up their hammocks, they strip off sweat-soaked clothes before inspecting their skin for ticks – picking off the bloated bodies. Supper is a mix of rations and whatever has been caught that day – iguana lizard (which tastes like rubbery chicken), wild turkey, rank monkey. The conversation inevitably turns to a grumbling discussion about yet another soul-destroying day, progressing just a few hundred metres deeper into the rainforest. The team had first entered the dense jungle seventeen days ago, and yet in that time they had covered just 50 kilometres. There are 320 kilometres to go.

The jungle was a cruel adversary. Day after day, expedition members blasted and hacked their way through endless vegetation. Scouts ventured out on recces, trying to find the easiest route to clear a path for the pack horses and vehicles. Explosives were used to tear apart the most stubborn greenery before engineers attacked it with machetes and power saws. 'The jungle is consuming us mentally and physically,' wrote expedition leader Colonel John Blashford-Snell. 'We are rapidly becoming enslaved by the Gap.'

It was 1972. Blashford-Snell was leading a large expedition supported by the British Army, with the aim of being the first to complete the Pan-American Highway. This 48,000-kilometre-long route stretches from Alaska to Cape Horn at the tip of South America and is the world's longest drivable road; one long paved route all the way from north to south, except for one break – the Darién Gap.

Also known as 'El Tapon' ('The Stopper'), this 100- by 160-kilometre swathe of merciless jungle remains virtually out of bounds. Back in the 1500s, the Spanish tried to settle there, but indigenous tribes torched sites and drove the conquistadors away. Then, in the 1690s, Scotland attempted to start a colony, but this again failed.

Rafting a Range Rover during the crossing of the Darién Gap

Despite the technological age we live in today, still no roads or major settlements exist inside its tropical walls. The sole residents are around 2,000 indigenous Embera-Wounaan and Kuna people, who cross the challenging terrain on foot or by river in dugout canoes. However, the Darién Gap is notorious for dangerous drug traffickers and, every year, a stream of intrepid migrants enter this no-man's land on the long trek up to the Mexican–US border, intent on finding a new life in the States. As it's relatively easy to enter some South American countries from abroad, some of the migrants come from as far away as Africa or the Middle East. Despite the many challenges migrants have faced, the Darién Gap is seen as one of the most challenging parts to the journey.

Few vehicles have ever conquered this jungle hell. In 1960, a Jeep and a Land Rover succeeded in finding a route through. On board were anthropologist Reina Torres de Araúz and her cartographer husband,

Amado Araúz. When not wielding machetes, they were taking detailed notes, and the couple's research was key to establishing the Darién National Park, which is now a UNESCO World Heritage Site.

Blashford-Snell's expedition also made it through – but only just. Regularly, tree stumps ripped apart car tyres. During one stretch of the journey, thick mud broke a car axle and a spare part had to be shipped in from the UK and parachuted into a clearing in the jungle. On another occasion, a vehicle almost plummeted down a 20-metre-deep gorge. Tropical illnesses, such as trench foot, harangued team members. Pack horses got ill and had to be put down. One team member had a lucky escape and was airlifted out after being bitten by a deadly snake.

Despite all the challenges, one aspect of the expedition was a huge success. Supported by the Natural History Museum, the scientists on the expedition gained an invaluable insight into the huge biodiversity of this area of virgin jungle, home to all sorts of species: huge dragonflies, tiny frogs, vicious vipers, armies of ants, bird-eating spiders the size of dinner plates, wild pigs called peccaries, giant sharp-toothed otters, colourful kingfishers, elegant egrets, crafty caiman, and the much feared 'tiger' – the local word for jaguar.

But the Darién Gap remains one of the least scientifically explored regions on Earth – a potential botanic treasure trove of undiscovered creatures and plants, hoarding remedies to combat diseases.

Many hope that it will remain this way. A road to connect the Pan-American Highway would bring tourists and trade, threatening indigenous cultures, accelerating deforestation and spreading disease – so far, nature's wall has kept foot-and-mouth cattle disease from spreading up to North America.

Even as an experienced explorer, Blashford-Snell described ploughing through this untamed wilderness as the toughest challenge of his career. 'More than once we thought we wouldn't make it,' he wrote. But, ninety-nine days after first entering its green walls, the expedition emerged. 'Without warning, the jungle ended and we stepped on to the beaten earth road that led to Lomas de Rumié.' Once they arrived in nearby Barranquillito, the team partied into the early hours, relieved to have survived the horrors of the jungle. From there, they headed south, making it all the way down to the tip of South America. Conquering the Darién Gap was surely the most challenging section, and was described as one of the most ambitious projects ever undertaken by the British Army. The route they hacked through the jungle became known to the indigenous people as *Carretera Inglese* – the Englishman's Highway.

METEORITE HUNTER

As the sun sets over the Australian Outback, the flies cease their constant buzzing and all is calm at last. Monica Grady takes off her wide-brimmed hat, which she'd covered with netting to keep the pests at bay, and then stretches out after a long, hot day in the desert. 'It was incredible to sleep out under the stars – except that I'm so short-sighted, I had to keep my glasses on to look at them as I drifted off to sleep,' joked Grady.

Born in Leeds in 1958, the eldest of eight children, Grady is now a professor of planetary and space science at the Open University, where she has worked on missions such as the *Beagle 2* project to Mars and the Rosetta comet mission.

In 2002, Grady was part of an expedition to the Nullarbor in Western Australia to hunt for meteorites – lumps of rocky material found on the surface of Earth that have come from space (as opposed to meteors that burn up in the atmosphere).

There are three main types of meteorites: stony meteorites, which are mostly made up of silicate minerals; stony-iron meteorites, which have similar amounts of metal and silicate crystals; and iron meteorites that are mostly made of metal.

At the moment, we can't journey to the centre of the Earth to find out more about the iron core. So iron meteorites are invaluable, because they give us an idea about what the inside of our planet is like and how many planets there may have been in the early solar system.

The Nullarbor is a good hunting ground, as its arid climate means that any iron meteorites don't rust. Also, any stony ones don't rot like they would if they landed in a more humid climate. Plus,

The metal detectorist

Antarctica is a meteorite gold mine. In the freezing yet dry climate, stony meteorites are often well preserved – and not too hard to find. Not only is the dark, rocky material easy to spot against the white wasteland, but meteorites move with the ice until they come up against a mountain chain, where they accumulate at its base – a bunch of them just waiting to be discovered. But finding iron meteorites in the Antarctic has always been tricky. This is because the iron heats up under the glare of the sun, and so any meteorites lying on the icy surface gradually melt through it, burying themselves.

Dr Katherine Joy, from the University of Manchester, has come up with an ingenious plan. Alongside the British Antarctic Survey (BAS), she has devised a metal detector to locate iron meteorites hidden within the ice. So far, the device has been tested in the Norwegian archipelago of Svalbard. But the BAS hopes to try it out at the UK's Halley Research Station in Antarctica in 2019.

the Nullarbor is an ancient desert, so it's been accumulating and preserving meteorites for many millions of years.

The team landed in Perth before driving for a couple of days across to Nullarbor, where they set up camp. After about two months' hard slog (and a bit of stargazing), they had collected around thirty meteorites. Incredibly, within just one square kilometre, over the course of a couple of days they discovered four meteorites – all different types. While the Nullarbor preserves meteorites well, no more of them land there than they do on other parts of the planet. This goes to show just how many meteorites must rain down on Earth – of course, many end up in the oceans that cover around two-thirds of the planet's surface. When a meteorite passes through the Earth's atmosphere, it becomes incandescently hot through frictional heating by the air, and the outer layer melts, creating a burnt-looking surface known as a fusion crust. Different types of meteorite have different types of fusion crust.

'I get particularly excited by meteorites with glossy fusion crusts,' said Grady. 'Because they're more rare and from asteroids like Vesta, which is unlike other asteroids in that it has a separate core and crust, like Earth does.'

After cataloguing all the meteorites collected on the expedition, the team sent them to the Australian Museum in Sydney for analysis; there they were weighed and then carefully cracked open to reveal their secrets.

Meteorites are like spaceships from other worlds as their composition reveals insights into the planets, comets and asteroids from which they originated. Expeditions like the one to Nullarbor provide important clues for understanding more about these worlds, and whether life could exist or has existed there once upon a time.

THE SUBTERRANEAN LOST WORLD

Rappelling down the 80-metre cliff face is like entering a prehistoric world. Above, light streams from the cave entrance, illuminating the behemoth cavern. Below awaits a lush, green jungle of thick foliage and 30-metre-tall trees. Touching down, the team hunt for a route through the undergrowth, exhilarated by what lies ahead.

Once out of the dense vegetation, they scramble on through darker passages. Eventually, the cave widens again. Across the cavern stands a huge 70-metre-tall stalagmite that looks a bit like a canine paw, which they nickname the Hand of Dog. The name sticks. They push on, reaching a ledge at the top of a long, steep slope of moss-covered terraces. Gazing out over the rugged terrain below, team member Jonathan Simms jokes to a colleague: 'Watch out for dinosaurs' – which becomes the name for that particular ledge.

Indeed, if there were a few dinosaurs prowling around, this could be a scene from Arthur Conan Doyle's *The Lost World*. But this is not some Amazonian plateau. It's the world's largest cave. There are other contenders around the planet for this title – some are longer, others deeper – but Hang Son Doong in Vietnam is the biggest known cave by volume.

At over 5 kilometres long, it has sections that stretch up to 200 metres tall and 150 metres wide – so vast that a forty-storey skyscraper could fit inside it and a Boeing 747 could fly through it. With its own subterranean river, two jungles, a beach (where visitors camp out overnight) and even its own microclimate, it is immense.

The cave was discovered in 1991 by a local boy, Ho Khanh, who was sheltering from a storm while out on a hunting trip. But, as Khanh forgot exactly where he'd stumbled across it, for a number of decades it lay hidden beneath the rugged Phong Nha-Ke Bang National Park, which is near the border with Laos. Then in 2009, the cave entrance was relocated, and this team of scientists were the first people to venture into its depths. It is part of a network of around 150 caves in the Annamite Mountains, many of which have never been surveyed.

Hang Son Doong formed somewhere between 2 and 5 million years ago when water tracing along a fault line in soft limestone rock scoured out the cave underground. However, where the limestone was too weak, the ceiling collapsed to form sinkholes, creating gigantic skylights that bathe parts of the cave in sunlight.

Hang Son Doong is filled with intriguing geological features: giant stalagmites and so-called 'cave pearls' – which form over centuries when dripping water builds up layers of calcite around sand grains. Some cave pearls in Hang Son Doong are the size of boulders.

It is also home to an abundance of wildlife. So far 154 mammals, 117 reptiles, 58 amphibians, 314 birds, 170 fish, including rare species, such as blind fish and Myriapoda centipedes, have been recorded. Seven of these species are endemic, so they don't exist anywhere else in the world.

On their first expedition, the team made it as far as a 60-metre-high wall of crumbling calcite, which they named the Great Wall of Vietnam, before they had to turn back, retracing their steps. Back across the knee-deep ditch of water, filled with sticky mud that sucks energy, and is called Passchendaele after the First World War battle where hundreds of thousands of Allied soldiers died just to gain a few kilometres of ground; back across the roaring subterranean river; back up through the Garden of Edam – another patch of dense jungle lying beneath a vast skylight; and back past the Watch Out for Dinosaurs and Hand of Dog.

This was the first of a number of expeditions by intrepid scientists and film crews. Currently, only a few hundred tourists are allowed in annually. But, in recent years, developers have been eyeing up more tourism opportunities. One idea is to string a cable car from the cave's roof, which would ferry in around 1,000 people every hour. Scientists are concerned. Such a scheme could severely damage this fragile ecosystem. Who knows what other beasts lie within its depths, just waiting to be discovered. And the risk is that, as more humans visit, species will go extinct before they have even been discovered.

THE COLDEST JOURNEY

The huge, red hull of SA *Agulhas* glides slowly under Tower Bridge in London before making its way down the Thames. Emblazoned in large white capitals along the side of the ship are the words 'Seeing is believing' – the name of the charity the expedition is raising money for.

On board the ship is a six-man team who are about to take on a challenge that no one has ever attempted before – to cross the Antarctic in the depths of winter. For years, such a journey at that time of year had been considered too perilous. Yet many explorers believed it to be the last true remaining polar challenge. Beforehand, the team knew what they'd be up against – a 3,200-kilometre slog across one of Earth's most hostile environments, in near permanent darkness, at temperatures dipping close to –90 degrees Celsius. It's no wonder the expedition was called The Coldest Journey.

The SA *Agulhas* arrived at Crown Bay in Antarctica in late January 2013, having made a pit stop in Cape Town on the way. After a number of weeks unloading gear and settling into life on the ice, the six-man team were ready to begin their epic journey. But then disaster struck.

Expedition leader Ranulph Fiennes – considered by many to be one of the greatest explorers of all time – got a serious case of frostbite in his left hand and had to make the tough decision to pull out. The remaining five men rallied together and eventually left camp in late March.

Aside from attempting to cross the continent during the Antarctic winter, the expedition aimed to study the physical and psychological effects on the human body in such an extreme environment. The team was certainly up against it: bitterly cold temperatures, almost constant darkness that messed with their natural day/night body clocks, isolation from the rest of humanity (with no chance of evacuation during the Antarctic winter), and altitudes up to 3,200 metres (in fact, the extreme cold and low gravitational field at high latitudes reduces the atmospheric pressure, creating low oxygen levels that you'd typically find at 3,800 metres).

Before setting off, they'd all undergone checks at King's College London, such as tests on eyesight, cardio-respiratory fitness, muscle strength, VO2 max, and a full body scan. These results were to be compared with tests performed during and after the expedition, such as blood, urine and stool samples, and eye tests (photos of the eye taken using a smartphone).

The team members knew the expedition would push them to their limits, but no one could have known quite what lay ahead. Not far into the expedition, treacherous deep crevasses and compacted 'blue' ice had become the norm. Even their two Caterpillars were unable to plough through the 2-metre-high banks of ice. On top of this, the team started to realize that they were dicing with death – the numerous crevasses posed a very real danger of suddenly swallowing up their tents without warning. It was time to call it a day and turn back.

As the team headed back to the coast, instead they focused on the scientific experiments they'd been tasked with, such as taking snow samples at different camps and daily meteorological readings, as well as more specific experiments like testing pain tolerance – which involved dipping fingers in ice baths. But team member Ian Prickett says the toughest element of the expedition was the psychological challenge: 'The hardest was living in a small enclosed space with four other men who didn't always see eye to eye.'

Prepping for Mars

A journey to Mars would take around six to eight months. Aside from the physiological effects on the human body of making such a journey (see page 214), one of the biggest challenges would be how crew would cope psychologically with the isolation.

While The Coldest Journey set out to test this on an expedition across the extreme world of Antarctica, other projects have also looked at how humans would deal with living in a small team in an isolated environment, cut off from civilization.

The Mars 500 project locked a team of six men in a windowless habitat in Moscow for 520 days. More recently, the NASA HERA base in the Johnson Space Center, HI-SEAS habitat in Hawaii, the NASA Extreme Environment Mission Operations (NEEMO) underwater Aquarius lab in Florida, the Concordia base in Antarctica, and the Mars Desert Research Station (MDRS) in the Utah desert have all acted as Mars-mission analogues.

The MDRS base was chosen for its close resemblance to the planet's terrain, and has a permanent habitat, science dome and observatory, where team members carry out experiments and conduct 'spacewalks' out into the desert. Only by studying both the human body *and mind* in isolated environments like these will we be prepared for a voyage to Mars.

A key part of the project was to analyse the psychological state of each team member – by keeping mood diaries – with a view to applying results to future manned missions to other planets, such as Mars.

So, while the expedition wasn't a resounding success, as the team had to turn back and didn't manage to cross the great icy desert, their scientific studies and insights into the human mind when under huge duress in a remote environment have proved invaluable.

As the president of the US Mars Society, Robert Zubrin, said: 'The expedition is a bold move that will add significantly to our understanding of how to deal with the challenge of human exploration of the Red Planet.'

XTREME EVEREST

Ahead lies a vast flood plain, with a few fields of barley down by the river and a scattering of mud-brick homes. The team trudge on. It's a number of days' trek to Everest base camp, with high passes to navigate over. As the days pass, civilization dwindles to just a few isolated nomadic camps. The team pass the occasional group of crows feeding on the remains of a dead body – the Buddhist tradition of a 'sky burial'. The landscape changes to treeless, scrubby vegetation, crisscrossed with powerful rivers. At last, the base campe comes into view – a montage of brightly coloured tents, scattered among rocks at the foot of the Khumbu Icefall. This is to be the team's home for the next few weeks.

After a night recovering, these intrepid doctors and scientists get to work, setting up the lab. This consists of a few green military-style tents crammed with desks, chairs, laptops, medical devices and exercise bikes. It's March 2013. The aim of this Xtreme Everest 2 expedition is to investigate why some people cope better in low oxygen conditions than others, in order to help patients in intensive care units back home. Around 90 per cent of patients in intensive care suffer from low levels of oxygen, a condition known as hypoxia. Untreated, hypoxia can lead to death, yet current treatments involve invasive and aggressive methods, such as using strong drugs to make the heart pump faster, which risks damaging the organ. New techniques are needed. But testing these on critically ill patients isn't an option. By analysing the human body at altitude, where oxygen levels are lower, the aim is to find other ways to treat hypoxia in hospital settings.

The first Xtreme Everest expedition took place back in 2007. It was the largest high-altitude research experiment ever conducted, involving about 200 people, split into groups of fourteen. Around twenty-four of them made it to the summit of Everest, but the main aim of the expedition was to conduct a battery of sixty-odd tests at different altitudes – first of all in a lab in London, then at 3,500 metres, then at base camp at 5,380 metres.

All the results were intriguing. The amount of oxygen in the blood didn't seem to make a difference to performance. When two participants were compared, the fit, ultra-marathon runner fared worse (and had to be evacuated by helicopter at 5,300 metres) than the much less fit person who made it to the summit. The length of time at altitude also didn't seem to matter; the results were no different whether someone had spent eight weeks acclimatizing or if they had just arrived. Nor did it make a difference what age or gender they were. The key finding was to do with nitric oxide (NO) in the blood.

The highest unclimbed mountain

At 7,570 metres, Gangkhar Puensum is only the world's fortieth-highest mountain, but no one has ever made it to the top – partly because of its location. It sits somewhere on the Bhutan-Tibetan border, but its exact location is still up for debate because the boundary line is disputed. Chinese maps draw the peak on the border, while others put the summit in Bhutan. There have been four proper attempts to reach the top. The first in 1985 came unstuck when they couldn't actually find the summit – maps of the area were somewhat sketchy until relatively recently. Subsequent attempts to scale the peak were hindered by frostbite and strong winds. Then, in 1994, before anyone else could have a go, Bhutan banned climbing of peaks any higher than 6,000 metres, reportedly to respect local spiritual beliefs. In 1998, a Japanese team tried to skirt the ban by scaling the mountain from the Chinese side. But the Bhutan government got wind of the expedition and put pressure on the Chinese to revoke the team's climbing permit. To this day, Gangkhar Puensum remains unconquered.

NO is a naturally occurring molecule, which is used by the body in various ways, helping to widen blood vessels and to control mitochondria – the power packs of cells. The researchers found that the higher the altitude, the more NO existed in the blood, and people who had been to high altitude before had higher levels during the expedition's ascent than those who had never climbed so high.

So, when the team returned to base camp five years later, further NO research was one of their key focuses. A different lot of around 200 people were involved in the 2013 expedition, but this time the groups were also made up of Sherpas.

Sherpa are an ethnic group who live in mountainous regions of Nepal and other areas of Asia, but the term is often used to refer to mountain guides or porters. They are renowned for being able to cope better in low oxygen conditions. The 2013 expedition aimed to unravel Sherpa secrets by comparing their physiology and genetics with 'lowlanders'.

Other studies had found that Sherpa blood NO levels are higher, and that their hearts pump more quickly yet use slightly different substances for this. Most intriguing of all is their red blood cell count. Red blood cells carry oxygen around the body. As a lowlander acclimatizes, the number of red blood cells typically increases. Yet Sherpa have fewer red blood cells than the average lowlander, although those cells are able to carry more oxygen.

The 2013 Xtreme Everest 2 expedition tests went a step further. Analysis of mitochondria from muscle tissue samples showed that Sherpa not only use oxygen more efficiently to make ATP (an energy-carrying molecule found in the cells of all living things), but also that energy levels in their muscles increase at altitude, when that of lowlanders drop. There are still many unanswered questions, but pharmaceutical companies are now working with the Xtreme Everest researchers to develop new drugs to treat hypoxia.

The final chapter in this project took place in 2017 when some of the team flew out to Kathmandu and travelled on to Namche Bazaar. Gathered inside the monastery were many from the local community, including the Sherpa who had taken part in the 2013 research expedition. They listened intently as the team revealed their results from the latest expedition, which highlighted the Sherpa superpowers that have helped so many lowlanders to conquer the world's highest mountain.

THE CAVE OF CRYSTALS

Climbing into the ice-filled suits and strapping on their backpacks, the research team prepare to enter the hostile underworld. They step on to the platform and the lift shudders as they descend 300 metres down the mine shaft, before shuffling through the dark tunnel lit by their head torches. Just outside the cave, they don face masks, which are hooked up to ice-filled backpacks that provide a steady stream of cool air to their lungs. Then, squeezing through the gap, they enter the cavern.

The Cave of Crystals is an incredible sight to behold. Two storeys in height and the size of a football field, it is filled with gigantic beams of gypsum – many over a metre wide and up to 15 metres in length. These are the largest known crystals in the world.

Geologists think that the crystals have grown so huge because the conditions are just right. Around 26 million years ago, scalding-hot magma forced its way up through a fault, depositing metals like gold, silver, zinc and lead in the limestone bedrock above. But some caverns were flooded with groundwater, which dissolved the limestone, creating calcium that combined with sulphur in the water to form crystals. Nonetheless, for crystals to grow so enormous they need lots of time, which is what they've had – millions of years cocooned in this subterranean cavern, as it was discovered only relatively recently.

Mining in the Chihuahua area of Mexico started back in the early nineteenth century. As groundwater was pumped out of the cave system, the miners were able to explore ever deeper inside one of the cave systems known as the Naica Mine. What they discovered astounded them.

In 1910, they stumbled upon a cavern whose walls were covered

Gypsum crystals inside the Naica cave

with blade-like gypsum crystals up to a metre in length. It was named Cueva de las Espadas, meaning the Cave of Swords.

But the Cave of Crystals lay undetected for almost another ninety years. In April 2000, brothers Eloy and Javier Delgado had been tasked with excavating a new tunnel in the Naica Mine for the Peñoles mining company, but what they opened up was a window into a truly magical world. As Eloy clambered through a small hole and entered the cavern, it was like stepping into a blast furnace – his clothes immediately became drenched in sweat. But the sight before him was like none ever seen before – huge beams of crystals lay scattered haphazardly around the cave, as if a giant had had fun hurling them around. He knew he had discovered something special.

Today, only a few people have been lucky enough to experience the awe of this cave in real life. For a long time, the Peñoles mining company kept it a secret to protect it from vandalism. And so it's been made accessible to only a few intrepid researchers and the odd journalist. With temperatures of up to 60 degrees Celsius and humidity over 90 per cent, this is truly one of the most inhospitable places on Earth. Even custom-made suits and ice-filled backpacks protect visitors for just a short period of time – any longer than an hour in the cave and you risk not coming out alive.

But for the researchers of the latest expedition, the risk was worth it. In 2017, they discovered microorganisms that were new to science. The bizarre microbes were actually living inside the crystals, surviving in a semi-dormant state in pockets of liquid, possibly for around 50,000 years. The pitch-black cave means the microbes had no sunlight from which to generate energy through photosynthesis, so instead they had survived through chemosynthesis – deriving their energy from chemical reactions.

This discovery begs the question of what other strange creatures may be lurking in the depths of the Naica Mine. We're unlikely to ever find out though. After debating whether to open the cave to the public, the Peñoles mining company decided that the extreme environment and inaccessibility meant it wouldn't be viable for tourism, so they have recently stopped pumping out groundwater from this section of the mine and let the cave re-flood. So, once more, the treasures of the Cave of Crystals lie cocooned in their watery subterranean world.

PART 2

UNCHARTED SEAS

Viewed from space, about 71 per cent of the Earth's surface is covered in water and, for centuries, humans have been casting off to explore the high seas. In the early days, inventions such as the marine chronometer helped us explore uncharted waters. As sea routes opened up, scientific exploration expanded with voyages such as Darwin's trip on HMS *Beagle*. Today, research crews sail the seas to better understand Earth's oceans and climate in the hope of protecting its fragile ecosystems.

HOW AMERICA GOT ITS NAME

Maybe it was meeting Christopher Columbus in Seville in 1496, or simply his lust for adventure that drove Amerigo Vespucci to pack up his business and set sail for foreign lands. Whatever the reason, the businessman-turned-explorer was key in changing our understanding of the world map.

Vespucci was born in Florence in 1454 to a wealthy family, friends of the Medicis, who ruled the city for centuries. After moving to Seville in 1492, along with another Italian, Gianetto Berardi, he started a business kitting out ships for explorers.

This was the Age of Exploration, when nations, intent on hunting for riches abroad and laying claim to foreign lands, sent adventurous explorers to the ends of the Earth. The ones who returned home brought back ships laden with gold, silver and gems – and tales of exotic lands.

With his business going down the pan and swept up in the romantic fever of adventure, Vespucci himself wanted to go exploring. This is where the story becomes somewhat murky. Most accounts claim that he set sail west for the New World in 1499. But a letter written in 1497 suggested he'd been on a previous voyage and hit mainland America before Columbus. The majority of sources claim the letter to be a fake.

Whatever the truth, at the time, everyone – including Columbus – thought that the Americas were part of Asia. On his voyage in 1499, when Vespucci hit land and sailed up the Amazon River, he believed he was exploring the eastern coastlines of Asia – and gave names to places such as the Gulf of Ganges.

It wasn't until his next voyage, in 1501, that he began to question whether these new lands were in fact Asian at all. Sailing down the coast of Patagonia, he saw things that really didn't fit with the descriptions from explorers such as Marco Polo. The people didn't look like the paintings he'd seen, the fruits didn't taste like the ones he'd heard about. Gradually, it dawned on him that this was a whole new continent. Vespucci is credited with being the first person to recognize that North and South America were different continents to Asia.

But he didn't actually give America its name. That was proposed by German clergyman Martin Waldseemüller. In 1507, the amateur cartographer published a map labelling a state in South America as 'America' – the feminine version of Amerigo. The name has existed ever since.

Vespucci the scientist

Vespucci also deserves to be recognized for his contributions to science, as on his voyages he made a number of discoveries. He realized that the constellations in the night sky that were visible in other parts of the world were different to the ones in Europe, which led to improved techniques in celestial navigation.

For centuries, travellers had navigated using stars as reference points. Although they could not measure longitude (the angular distance of a place east or west of the Greenwich meridian), they could measure latitude – the distance north or south of the equator. Latitude was calculated using a device called an astrolabe, which measured the angle of the sun or a star above a horizontal line of reference, such as the horizon.

A talented cartographer, Vespucci drew up maps of the lands he visited. And, incredibly for the time, he estimated the circumference of the Earth to within 80 kilometres of its actual size.

PROVING EARTH IS ROUND

NASA not only faked the moon landings, but also that iconic image of the round Earth taken from the moon. Or so say 'flat-earthers' – people who believe that our planet isn't round, despite us having known for over 2,000 years that it is.

For centuries, Mediterraneans and Mesopotamians had believed that Earth was a coin-shaped disc with the Mediterranean Sea at the centre of a land mass, which was surrounded by seas stretching to the edges of the world. The idea that Earth was not flat was first raised by Greek philosopher Pythagoras around 500 BC. He didn't have any scientific evidence to go on, just an inkling that the gods would have designed the world as a sphere.

Around a century later, another Greek philosopher, Plato, came up with the idea that there must be a large land mass on the other side of the sphere – to balance it out. But, again, this had no scientific basis. Indeed, anyone with an ounce of common sense would have thought these philosophers to be mad. How on earth (literally) could objects stay on the ground if they were upside down on the underside of the sphere?

It was one of Plato's students, Aristotle, who first came up with the scientific rationale for a round Earth. Through watching the night sky, he observed that star constellations rose in the sky as travellers ventured south, and that different sets of stars appear depending on where you are – those in the northern hemisphere differ to the ones in the south. If the Earth was flat, the whole world would see the same stars at the same time.

Aristotle also spotted that the Earth's shadow on the moon was circular during a lunar eclipse. It was a revolutionary breakthrough in our understanding of the planet we live on. But, it was to be many hundreds of years before someone actually navigated their way all around the globe.

Portuguese-born navigator Ferdinand Magellan spent his early maritime years voyaging to places like Morocco and Malaysia. But it was working for the Spanish that made him his name.

In 1519, Magellan and his 270 men set sail on five ships across the Atlantic. The goal was to find a western sea route to the Spice Islands in Indonesia, via the fabled water passage across South America, which would avoid the perilous Cape Horn at the tip of the continent.

But, after months of searching along Brazilian estuaries, many of the starving crew mutinied, almost getting the better of Magellan. However, by killing one ship's captain and ditching another, he managed to survive – and eventually found the passage that cut off the tip of South America. It is now known as the Strait of Magellan.

It took around a month to navigate along the 560-kilometre-long waterway but, when the ships emerged, it was the first time that any European had ever seen the Pacific Ocean. Amazed by how calm it was compared to the rough waters of the strait, Magellan named it Mar Pacifico. Whether he felt the same about it many months later is another matter. He hadn't anticipated it would be quite so vast. With food supplies depleted, Magellan was lucky to avoid another revolt from his starving crew.

But, finally, in March 1521, his remaining ships hit land in Guam, recovering momentarily before limping on to the Philippines. Buoyed up by surviving the voyage, Magellan tried to convert the local people to Christianity. Most were having none of it and Magellan ended up with a poison arrow lodged in his right leg. He died from the wound on 27 April 1521.

With Magellan out of the picture, crew member Sebastian del Cano took command of the remaining two ships and eventually

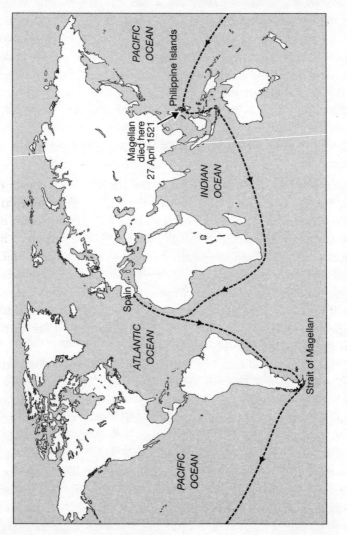

The expedition route. Only one of the original five ships returned to Spain

made it back to Seville, three years and one month after setting off. While Magellan himself didn't circumnavigate the globe, he is recognized as having led the first expedition to do so. The mission that set out to find a western sea route to the Spice Islands ended up proving that the world is indeed round and bigger than anyone had previously imagined.

THE PIRATE PLANT COLLECTOR

Lying low on the sand, William Dampier crawls closer to the turtle. The moon illuminates the great beast, unaware of its audience – so wrapped up in methodically scooping away the sand with its back flippers to create a hole. The stars come out. And the turtle begins to lay its eggs – tens of them. Once done, it carefully covers them over with sand, then lumbers back to the water. Dampier retreats slowly back up the beach. This was just one of the many incredible experiences Dampier had on his first round-the-world voyage, which started in 1679.

Dampier was an explorer and navigator who made occasional forays into piracy. Born in Somerset in 1651, he was orphaned at a young age. With little to keep him in England and intent on adventure, he set sail for more exotic lands.

Initially, he worked on a sugar plantation in Jamaica. It was while in the Caribbean that Dampier had his first turtle encounter. In the seventeenth century, few Europeans had ever seen a turtle, let alone watched one lay eggs. Dampier recorded the whole process, writing about it in his book *A New Voyage Round the World*. The book went on to become a bestseller and was the first great travel journal in English, but also an incredible insight into the natural world. Indeed, it took the armchair traveller along for the ride, revealing insights into exotic lands, local peoples and intriguing wildlife.

In one chapter, Dampier describes the different turtles he encountered:

> The Trunk-Turtle is commonly bigger than the others, their backs are higher and rounder, and their flesh rank and not wholesome. The Loggerhead is so called because it has a huge head, much bigger than the other sorts ... The Hawksbill Turtle is the least kind. They are so called because their mouths are long and small, somewhat resembling the bill of a hawk.

He went on to reveal in detail their nesting behaviour, while also providing descriptions of their eggs and the key locations where they laid them.

While in the Caribbean, Dampier also encountered all sorts of other wildlife, such as humming birds and manatees.

> The manatee delights to live in brackish water and they are commonly in creeks and rivers near the sea. They live on grass of a narrow blade. Their flesh is white and extraordinarily wholesome. This creature is about the bigness of a horse ... The mouth of it is much like the mouth of a cow, having great thick lips. The eyes are no bigger than a small pea ...

He described the hummingbird as 'a pretty little feathered creature, no bigger than a great, over-grown wasp', and the armadillo as having 'a nose like a pig ... on any danger ... she lies stock-still like a land-turtle. And though you toss her about she will not move herself'.

From the Caribbean, Dampier moved on to Mexico, where he initially earned his keep in the logging industry. But it was while there that he ended up getting in with a bad crowd – a group of buccaneers whose pirate life promised a healthy income as well as a chance to see more of the world.

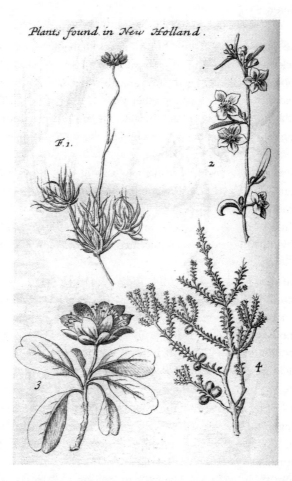

Plants found in New Holland.

Drawings by Dampier of plant species from modern-day Australia

From Central America he journeyed south, before heading west to the Galapagos Islands and then to the Far East – only returning to England twelve years after first setting off. When not pillaging precious cargo from ships bound for Europe, he collected plants and spent hours observing birds and beasts.

In the Far East, Dampier came across some truly bizarre species: 'sucking-fish' and 'flying foxes'. Flying foxes were huge bats 'with bodies as big as ducks'.

I judge that the wings stretched out in length, could not be less asunder than seven or eight foot from tip to tip; for it was much more than any of us could fathom with our arms extended to the utmost ... The skin or leather of them has ribs running along it; and there are sharp and crooked claws, by which they may hang on anything.

Dampier was a man who started out life with an adventurous streak and ended up a naturalist, cataloguing creatures and collecting plants from all over the world. But, aside from the meagre amounts he earned from his travel books, he mostly made his money through piracy.

While piracy has been rife for centuries, its heyday was in the late 1600s and early 1700s. The end of a lengthy war in Europe left many in the navy out of a job, which meant a number of unemployed yet skilled seamen turned their attention to treasure-laden boats returning from the New World and Far East. After a successful first voyage, he was invited to lead a scientific expedition to Australia – then known as New Holland or Terra Australis. The famous Shark Bay in Western Australia was named by Dampier because of the huge numbers of sharks in its waters. This second round-the-world trip was followed by a third circumnavigation of the globe, which set up his retirement after he seized a Spanish treasure ship.

Although Dampier was indeed a pirate, this legacy has possibly eclipsed his other work. In his lifetime, the explorer sailed more than 300,000 kilometres and encountered many mysterious lands, peoples and creatures. He was first and foremost a great naturalist.

FLOATING LABORATORIES

While France and England battled it out in Europe in the Napoleonic Wars, Frenchman Nicolas Baudin was tasked by Napoleon with exploring remote lands on the other side of the globe. The target: Terra Australis, also known as New Holland and now modern-day Australia. The aim: to collect living and preserved specimens of animals and plants, particularly unknown species that could be transplanted to France or its colonies to be exploited commercially.

Baudin came from humble beginnings, joining the merchant navy at the age of fifteen. Over the years he grew into an experienced naval officer, voyaging to distant lands. But Terra Australis was to be his most remote destination yet.

In October 1800, he set sail with his crew split between two ships – *Le Géographe* and *Le Naturaliste*. On board were twenty-four scientists, ranging from zoologists to botanists, geographers to astronomers. The vessels were like floating laboratories, laden with all sorts of scientific gadgets and gizmos. Some of these instruments were to help with navigation, such as the chronometer (see box). Others were for conducting experiments once they reached their destination. The dynamometer was a particularly bizarre contraption. Designed to measure the muscular strength

The chronometer

Today, many people have lost the ability to navigate by anything other than sat nav, while sailors are spoilt with the amount of high-tech equipment on board. But, in the early 1700s, sailors relied solely on the magnetic compass to navigate. Even with this device, they didn't know how far west or east they were, and so struggled to calculate their longitude. They were forced to sail north or south to the latitude of their destination, and then head directly west or east and hope they eventually hit land. But this all changed when English clockmaker John Harrison invented the marine chronometer – a very accurate and portable clock that allowed sailors to compare its time with that of another clock and so work out their longitude – which revolutionized navigation.

of both animals and humans, the plan was to use it to calculate the hand and (reputedly) the loin strength of different people they encountered on their travels. To accommodate all these gadgets, extra bodies and a large library of zoological textbooks, maps and charts, the vessels were adapted by removing some guns and adding an extra deck up above.

Despite all this extra weight, the ships eventually made it to Terra Australis. For many months they explored the western and southern coasts of the continent, mapping the region, collecting specimens, learning from the indigenous people as to how to cultivate certain plants, and making detailed sketches and notes on the exotic landscapes and creatures they encountered.

But one encounter was surely to stick in Baudin's memory – meeting Englishman Matthew Flinders. Captaining the aptly named

The Investigator, Flinders had been sent by the English to also explore Terra Australis. The two captains met in 1802 in what is now known as Encounter Bay. Their meeting was fairly friendly, but the state of politics at that time meant there was a serious rivalry between the two men – both wanted to bring glory to their nations by taking home invaluable scientific knowledge.

In the end, the Frenchman came out victorious with the haul of species he collected on the trip. Over 100,000 animals were amassed, including 125 mammals, 53 reptiles, 912 birds and over 4,000 insects, making it the largest number collected on any European trip. In those days, animals were seen as commodities to fill public zoos or private collections.

The aim was to get creatures back alive, but that wasn't always possible. On the return journey, Baudin ordered some scientists and officers to vacate their cabins, so that there would be enough room for the kangaroos and emus that he'd picked up. The seasick creatures were force-fed but some emus died. The descendents of the ones that survived now live in Paris's botanical garden, Jardin des Plantes.

It wasn't just animals that died on the journey. The likes of dysentery and tuberculosis claimed the lives of many of the crew, including the captain, who died of a nasty case of tuberculosis on a stopover at Île de France.

But the crew that did make it back had incredible tales to tell of exotic places. And the scientists had treasures never seen before in Europe. Dried plant specimens were taken to the Museum of Natural History in Paris. Live plant species were analysed for their useful properties – aromatic oils, dyes, medicinal remedies. And the detailed sketches and notes were catalogued in the annals of science, a window into life in those foreign lands.

THE GREAT NORTHERN EXPEDITION

White as the snow around, the furry beast inches closer to the limp hand. Its large ears twitch, yet it shows little fear. Perhaps that is because it has little *to* fear – what is left of the group are too weak to waste energy on chasing away an Arctic fox as it nibbles on the hand of a dead comrade. Huddled in makeshift holes dug into snow drifts, the shipwrecked crew fend off the creatures as best they can. Marooned on a bitterly cold desolate island for months, one by one death claims victims, including eventually the expedition leader, Vitus Bering – after whom the island is now named.

This tumultuous story first started over a decade before. In 1725, Bering had been tasked with finding a northern sea route between Siberia and the fabled 'Great Land' – modern-day Alaska. The trip was the brainchild of Russian ruler Peter the Great, who was intent on solidifying his stranglehold on Siberia and finding new trade routes to the east. So Bering set out from St Petersburg and traipsed thousands of kilometres across Russia, making it as far as the Pacific Ocean. After building a boat, he set sail up the east coast, but bad weather drove him back.

Undaunted, Bering returned a decade later – but this time with a vast retinue made up of scientists, soldiers, servants and some of their families. Never had such a grand expedition been undertaken, and it cost Peter the Great dearly – over one-sixth of the empire's annual income.

After four years trudging 8,000 kilometres across the Siberian wilderness, the expedition finally arrived on the east coast at Okhotsk, where Bering built two ships for the journey into uncharted waters. Little did the crews of the *St Peter* and *St Paul* know what they were about to endure – a voyage so arduous that not many would return.

Both ships made it across what is now the Bering Sea to Alaska for the summer of 1741. But on the return journey raging storms, blinding blizzards and thick fog split the two parties. The *St Paul* made it back to Siberia by October (minus a number of crew who succumbed to scurvy), but the *St Peter* fared far worse – a wild storm wrecking the ship and marooning the crew on the desolate Bering Island.

On board was Bering as well as a German-born naturalist by the name of Georg Steller. While others weakened and some died, Steller got lucky and stayed healthy – and ended up making the most of his time trapped on the island over the winter. For a naturalist, the barren island was anything but barren, with all sorts of birds and beasts on land and in the coastal waters. Some were previously unknown to science, such as the enormous, bulbous manatee.

Steller described the creature as 'agreeably yellow as the best Holland butter'. This species grew up to 2 metres in length and weighed up to 600 kilos – the size of a small whale. But the docile creature was relatively easy to catch. Alongside birds like the spectacled cormorant, the manatee provided the marooned crew with enough food to see them through the worst of the bitter winter.

Indeed, Steller foresaw a time when hoards of hunters would follow in the expedition's footsteps and come in search of the creatures for their beef-tasting meat and valuable skins. And he was right: within a few decades, hunters had forced this species into extinction.

As spring broke, the remaining crew constructed a small boat from the wreckage of the *St Peter* and eventually made it back to the Russian coast, ten months after being shipwrecked.

The expedition was both a huge success and a huge failure. Through surveying the uncharted coastline, Bering opened up a whole new region of the world – aiding global trade. Yet by doing so he signed the death warrant of some species as the hunters moved in. One such was the Steller manatee. Its namesake was the only naturalist ever to see and describe the mammal. In his book, *The Beasts of the Sea* (*De Bestiis Marinis*), published in 1751, Steller revealed how he and some of the other crew dissected one of the manatees on the beach on Bering Island.

The naturalist certainly left a legacy, with a number of species named after him: Steller's jay, Steller's sea eagle, the duck Steller's eider, the mollusc *Cryptochiton stelleri* and Steller's sea lion. And the Great Northern Expedition definitely achieved its goals of charting uncharted waters, opening up new trade routes and discovering new species. Yet at what cost to the lives of both the crew and the local wildlife.

CAPTAIN COOK'S SECRET MISSION

The year 1763 saw the end of the Seven Years' War, a conflict between almost every great European power. But as one conflict finished, another was about to begin. This time there was to be no hand-to-hand combat, but a fight between Britain, France, Spain, Portugal and the Netherlands to claim new territories around the world. The Pacific and South Seas were largely unexplored, yet the British needed to act fast if they wanted to lay claim to previously undiscovered lands. But to avoid other countries getting wind of their plans, the British government needed a decoy. Science was to provide one.

A few decades earlier, Astronomer Royal Edmond Halley (of Halley's Comet fame) had urged astronomers around the world to club together to try to solve one of the great scientific challenges of the century – to accurately calculate the size of the solar system.

Since the time of the Ancient Greeks, the distance between the sun and Earth had been worked out using various methods, some more accurate than others. But no one had come close to the correct figure. Halley realized that a transit of Venus across the sun would be a good chance to get an accurate calculation. Such a transit was rare, but there were two such events coming up within a decade of each other (in 1761 and 1769). Plus, the ambitious project would require amalgamating measurements from a number of different locations around the world.

Simultaneously observing the event at different places on the planet required plenty of manpower – and funding from governments. But the Seven Years' War was to hinder most attempts to observe the first transit in 1761. That just left the 1769 event as the last chance within their lifetimes.

When the Royal Society contacted the navy about organizing a voyage to the remote island of Tahiti in order to observe the 1769 transit, the British government spotted a chance. Under the guise of a scientific voyage, Britain could secretly scout around the Pacific for new territories to lay claim to.

Naval officer James Cook was tasked with this mission. In 1768, he set sail on HMS *Endeavour*, along with a ship full of astronomers, botanists and illustrators. The *Endeavour* lived up to its name, crossing the Atlantic, rounding the perilous Cape Horn at the tip of South America and arriving in Tahiti in time for the transit.

The astronomers managed to get a decent measurement and, when the expedition returned to Britain in 1771, their calculation helped work out the sun's distance to within 4 per cent of today's value. Not bad, considering the technology of the time.

After Tahiti, the *Endeavour* sailed south-west to New Zealand and on to Australia. A talented surveyor, Cook charted the whole coast of the two islands in just over six months. From there the ship sailed up the east coast of Australia, where the Great Barrier Reef blocked its path. Weaving carefully through the labyrinth of corals, the ship seemed to be making good progress. But on 11 June 1770 it ran aground off the coast of what is now known as Queensland, tearing a hole below the waterline, which nearly sank the ship. After being patched up, the vessel limped on, eventually undergoing full repairs in Java, Indonesia. It was in Java that dysentery and malaria claimed the lives of numerous crew.

Indeed, while a huge success, the expedition wasn't without its tragedies. En route to Tahiti, an exploration party became stranded in Tierra del Fuego on the barren tip of South America, where two servants died of exposure. Then in Tahiti, an illustrator died of an epileptic fit.

But when the *Endeavour* did finally return to British shores in 1771, its captain returned as something of a hero. Cook went on to captain several more expeditions. Indeed, in his lifetime, he discovered more of Earth's surface than any other person in history. And yet he came from a very humble background. The son of a farm worker, he worked as a coal merchant in Whitby in his teens before enlisting in the navy. His background may in fact be the reason he became so successful, rising up through the ranks, gaining popularity and respect by treating all men on his ship the same, whether they were scientists or ordinary sailors. He became one of the most famous explorers of all time. Yet by laying claim to new territories all around the globe, from South America to South Asia (often without the consent of the indigenous people), he was instrumental in the dubious accolade of 'the empire on which the sun never sets', which refers to how the sun was always shining on at least one territory in the British Empire that stretched around the globe at that time.

Banks the botanist

One of the scientists on board the *Endeavour* was a rising star of botany – Joseph Banks. Due to his personal wealth, Banks was able to part fund the trip in return for berths on board the ship, filling bunks with other botanists and artists who would help him collect, catalogue and illustrate species. In Tahiti, while the astronomers set up their telescopes ready for the big event, Banks and his compatriots busied themselves collecting specimens of all the island's birds and plants, as well as weapons and costumes produced by its indigenous people. By the time the ship docked back in Britain, on board were some 30,000 pressed and dried botanical specimens, including 1,400 species that were new to science. But, more than being a great botanist, Banks was also integral to all sorts of scientific discoveries both at home and abroad. While president of the Royal Society from 1778 until his death in 1820, he supported the careers of many scientists. He advised King George III on the development of Kew Gardens, and was integral to sending many botanists abroad to hunt for new plants, while turning the gardens into the centre of botanical research stations around the globe, and helping to introduce new crops and farming techniques across the British Empire.

ABOARD HMS *BEAGLE*

After a couple of false starts due to bad weather (and hangovers on Boxing Day), HMS *Beagle* set sail from Plymouth on 27 December 1831. On board the packed 27-metre-long ship were plenty of provisions and seventy-four people, including a young naturalist by the name of Charles Darwin.

Born in Shrewsbury in 1809, Darwin was from a young age obsessed with the natural world, exploring the countryside near his home and collecting all sorts of plants and bugs. While studying medicine at the University of Edinburgh, he was traumatized by watching surgery carried out on a child (anaesthetic didn't exist in those days), and promptly quit the course to study theology at Cambridge University instead. But, at the age of twenty-two, the opportunity of a lifetime came up – a chance to travel the world.

The *Beagle* followed the popular nineteenth-century shipping route from England to the Cape Verde Islands before striking west to modern-day Brazil, then down the coast of Argentina, where the adventures really got started – by the sea he collected fossils of enormous extinct mammals; and in the South American lowlands he journeyed overland on horseback, collecting specimens and meeting the wild horseman of the region, known as 'gauchos'. After exploring the east coast, the ship ventured on, successfully making it around the perilous Cape Horn to the relative sanctuary of Chile, where Darwin was among the crew to witness the violent eruption of Mount Osorno. From there, the ship headed on north, eventually reaching the Galapagos Islands.

Although these islands have gone down in history as being inextricably linked with Darwin's work, the ship actually stopped there for only five weeks – a small snippet in time considering the length of the epic five-year round-the-world trip. And, while he observed how the physiology of finches varied between the islands, there was no 'eureka' moment while in the Galapagos.

Nor was there a single light-bulb moment during any of the voyage. As he travelled the globe, the jottings in his 770-page diary and on his 1,750 pages of notes are evidence of how the exotic plants and animals that he encountered certainly challenged his thoughts about our place in the world. But it wasn't until the *Beagle* returned to England in 1836 that he started to consolidate his idea about natural selection – where organisms that are better adapted to an environment will survive and reproduce.

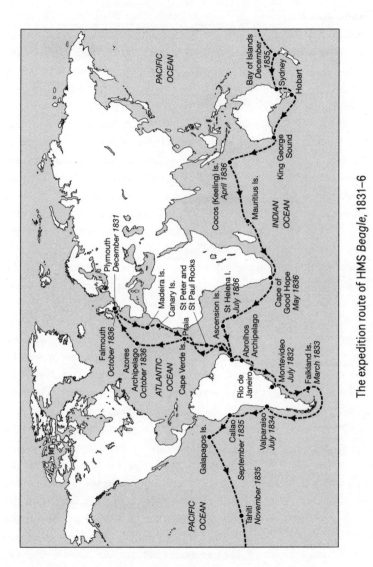

The expedition route of HMS *Beagle*, 1831–6

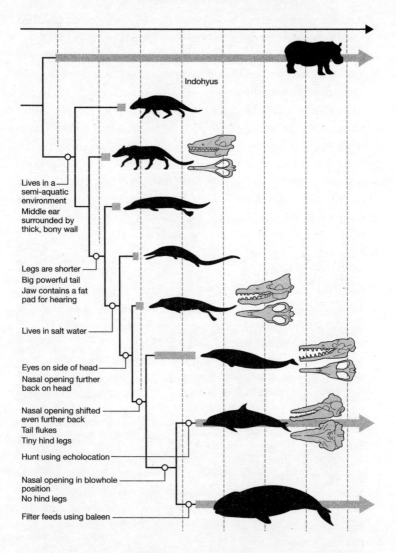

Indohyus

Lives in a
semi-aquatic
environment
Middle ear
surrounded by
thick, bony wall

Legs are shorter
Big powerful tail
Jaw contains a fat
pad for hearing

Lives in salt water

Eyes on side of head
Nasal opening further
back on head

Nasal opening shifted
even further back
Tail flukes
Tiny hind legs

Hunt using echolocation

Nasal opening in blowhole
position
No hind legs

Filter feeds using baleen

The evolution of whales

And it was to be another couple of decades before he published his then-controversial theory about evolution in *On the Origin of Species* – spurred on by competition from naturalist Alfred Russel Wallace who had written to him saying that he'd come to the same conclusion about evolution (see page 31).

Though Darwin is best remembered for his theory of natural selection, his time on the *Beagle* also helped with his contributions to other scientific theories, such as confirming Lyell's theory that geologic formations were the result of cumulative forces over eons of time, and coming to the (correct) conclusion that atolls formed when isolated rings of coral grew around extinct volcanoes that then sank into the sea.

Walking whales

When Darwin wrote the first edition of *On the Origin of Species* in 1859, he included a section on how natural selection could have caused a land mammal, such as a bear which caught insects in the water, to eventually evolve into a whale.

But his idea was ridiculed by the scientific establishment. So much so that he removed the section from the next edition. In fact, he wasn't far off the truth. Whales did indeed evolve from a four-legged land beast, but not a bear. The ancestor was actually a creature called *Indohyus*, which looked a bit like a mini deer and may have waded in the water like a hippo (see opposite).

During millions of years of evolution, the whale ancestors gradually lost their ability to walk on land – front legs evolved into flippers while back legs disappeared and tail flukes developed (although modern cetaceans still have traces of pelvises and very occasionally some are born with odd-shaped protrusions in the place of hind limbs).

By the time the *Beagle* returned to port in England, Darwin had amassed a vast collection of over 5,000 skins, bones and carcasses and 1,500 different species. Inevitably, the journey hadn't been without its mishaps and controversies. A recently discovered drawing from the time reveals a squabble that broke out on board the *Beagle* over Darwin's 'cursed' fossil and botanic specimens taking up too much space on the ship.

Still, Darwin described the voyage as 'by far the most important event in my life, and has determined my whole career … I feel sure that it was this training which has enabled me to do whatever I have done in science.' It was certainly instrumental in framing his theory of natural selection – one of the key building blocks in our understanding of the evolution of life.

HUNTING FOR THE MAGNETIC NORTH POLE

Huddled around the dying embers of the fire, the men tear off chunks of meat with their teeth. The Inuit hunters watch, intrigued. Gradually, the horror of what they are seeing dawns on them. Could that really be human meat? Appalled, they make their excuses and retreat across the ice. That was the last time that John Franklin and his men were ever seen alive.

Franklin was born in Spilsby, Lincolnshire, in 1786. He was just a teenager when, in 1800, he joined the Royal Navy aboard HMS *Polyphemus*. Two years later, he circumnavigated Terra Australis (modern-day Australia) with his cousin Matthew Flinders. (The same Flinders who met Baudin at Encounter Bay – see page 96.) A few years later, Franklin was the signals officer of HMS *Bellerophon* in the ferocious Battle of Trafalgar, which left him slightly deaf. After that, numerous voyages followed on land, sea and ice. But it was an

Arctic expedition that was to make him his name – and be the end of him.

Reports claim the expedition aim was to locate the Northwest Passage – the sea route through to the Pacific Ocean, via the Arctic. But this was a story dreamt up by Franklin's widow in an attempt to hide the truth about the demise of her husband, and make him out to be a hero explorer who gave his life for his country.

He did indeed sacrifice his life for a noble cause – a scientific endeavour. As a fellow of the Royal Society, Franklin's mission was to reach the magnetic north and carry out a nine-month-long series of observations on magnetic effects. It was part of a massive international effort to try to understand the Earth's magnetic field and see if it could be used to help with navigation. But getting to the magnetic north was no easy feat – even for an experienced sailor like Franklin.

In May 1845, HMS *Terror* and HMS *Erebus* cast off from London, with Franklin as captain. The two wooden warships had been reinforced to withstand the crushing pressure of sea ice. On board were 130 crew, as well as several tonnes of scientific equipment.

Greenland came and went. As did Beechey Island and Victory Point. Details of the voyage are sketchy. What we do know is that on 12 September 1846, the ships became stuck in the sea ice west of King William Island.

By this stage life on board was fairly dire. Aside from night-time temperatures of –48 degrees Celsius, the monotonous food of tinned food, salted meat and dried veg was running low. Tuberculosis and scurvy ravaged the crew. And Franklin himself eventually died on 11 June 1847. The rest of the crew ditched the ships and struck out across the ice in an attempt to reach the nearest trading post, 1,930 kilometres away. Malnourished and exhausted by years at sea, their efforts were futile. The survivors met a grisly end – eating their dead companions before eventually succumbing to the bleak wilderness.

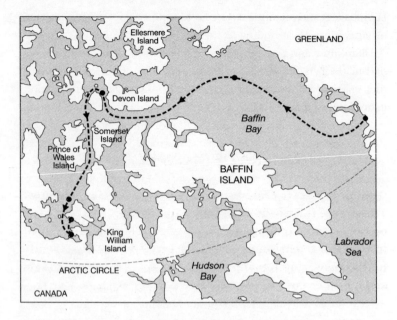

The route of HMS *Terror* and HMS *Erebus* from Greenland to
their final resting place

Some of the mysteries surrounding the expedition were solved
many years later when wrecks of the ships were found – HMS
Erebus in 2014 and HMS *Terror* two years later – along with skeletal
evidence of cannibalism. But evidence has also been found of a
research station, proving that Franklin had seen through his scientific
mission to discover the magnetic north and analyse magnetic effects.

Sadly, this has been forgotten in the annals of science. And
his widow was the culprit. In 1854, reports made their way to
Britain that Inuits had seen evidence of cannibalism. Distraught
by the suggestion that her husband would resort to such deeds,
Jane Franklin managed to rewrite the story to remove mentions of

cannibalism and scientific exploration, instead painting her husband as a hero, intent on finding a way through the Northwest Passage.

Franklin was a hero – a scientific hero. The scientist and explorer had made it his life's work to study magnetic effects. The irony is that we now know the Earth's magnetic core moves randomly, so cannot be used for navigation.

A NEW ERA OF GLOBAL COMMS

'I think my heart ceased to beat during those few minutes.' These were the words of engineer Daniel Gooch. It was early on the morning of Sunday, 2 September 1866. Silence reigned in the instrument room. The team were waiting impatiently for the answering signal from Ireland. At last it came through, and a new era of global communication began.

Real-time global communication is something that we take for granted today. But a couple of centuries ago, information moved across oceans at the speed of a sailing ship. Back in the mid-1800s, telegraph lines connected cities around the US, as well as Europe, even stretching across the seabed of the English Channel. Yet no such cable connected Europe with the US. With pressure from businesses, the challenge was on to lay a transatlantic telegraph cable.

Scientist Michael Faraday was well-known for his work on electromagnetism, having invented the electric motor, transformer and generator. He claimed that the enormous length of cable required to cross the Atlantic would limit the rate at which messages could be sent – now known as the 'bandwidth'.

Irish physicist William Thomson had other ideas. He thought that sufficiently high data rates could be achieved with a purer copper cable, which would conduct the electrical signal better, and provide more insulation around the cable, so that less electrical energy would be lost to the environment. Although this conflicted with the ideas of the Atlantic Telegraph Company's electrician Wildman Whitehouse, the company employed both men to work on the project. Confined to his sickbed, Whitehouse couldn't join the first cable-laying expedition in 1857. Thomson, however, was on board.

On 5 August, HMS *Agamemnon* and USS *Niagara* cast off from Valentia Island on the south-west coast of Ireland, both laden with huge lengths of cable, which wouldn't all fit on one ship. At first, things went according to plan, with some of the cable being successfully laid on the seafloor. But, later on that day, the cable broke apart and the expedition had to be abandoned.

Thomson went back to the drawing board, publishing in the *Engineer* his suggestions as to how to avoid such an accident again. And, in 1858, he developed a more sensitive version of the mirror galvanometer (see box) that could detect the weak signals emerging from the undersea cables, enabling faster messaging – where a character was received every 3.5 seconds.

The mirror galvanometer

A galvanometer detects electric currents, registering the strength of the current with a needle indicator. Thomson's mirror galvanometer had no needle. Instead, there was a mirror with a bar magnet cemented on the back, suspended on silk threads within the coil. A light was shone on the mirror and reflected on to a scale card a short distance away, which magnified any movement of the mirror. This meant that the mirror galvanometer was incredibly sensitive, and useful for detecting very weak electrical currents received on long submarine cables.

In 1858, a telegraph cable was successfully laid across the Atlantic, between Ireland and Newfoundland, over 2,000 nautical miles along a raised plateau on the seafloor. As one journalist described it: 'The Old and New Worlds are brought into instantaneous communication.' Indeed, Queen Victoria and the US President James Buchanan exchanged the first message via the cable: 'Upon the successful completion of this great international work … an additional link between the nations whose friendship is founded on their common interest and reciprocal esteem.' The message took sixteen hours to be relayed. However, it was a huge improvement on the time it would have taken beforehand, which was anything over ten days for a ship to cross the Atlantic.

But the cable wasn't ready for the demand. Whitehouse tried to improve the signal by boosting the voltage. Overloaded, the cable stopped working and communication ceased. However, businesses had sniffed the huge potential of a transatlantic telegraph cable – they weren't going to give up that easily.

The enormous steamship SS *Great Eastern*, designed by renowned engineer Isambard Kingdom Brunel, was converted specifically for laying cable, and another attempt was made in 1865. But disaster struck again when the cable broke halfway into the voyage, lost in the depths of the ocean.

Undeterred, the team tried again the following year – and their perseverance paid off. They not only managed to rescue the cable that was lost the previous year, but also succeeded in laying cable all the way across the Atlantic. And with the success of this feat, the world suddenly became a smaller place.

THE FIRST OCEANOGRAPHIC EXPEDITION

The leadsman hurls the weight into the water, watching as it quickly sinks below the waves, and the attached rope rapidly unfurls. Some of the crew gathered by his side make wagers on how deep it will sink. None realize that they are measuring the deepest part of the ocean anywhere in the world. It was the 1870s, and the crew were part of a great expedition that was the first true scientific voyage in history. It would lay the foundations of oceanography.

Back then, little was known about marine life and what lay in the ocean depths. Scottish marine zoologist Charles Wyville Thomson was a professor at the University of Edinburgh and fellow of the Royal Society when he came up with the idea of circumnavigating the globe to investigate the oceans. A good ship would be needed for such a task.

The Royal Society convinced the navy to lend them HMS *Challenger*, a warship that was adapted for its scientific voyage. The main aim of the expedition was to investigate the ocean at all sorts of different depths – collecting specimens of marine life and analysing samples from the surface down to the seabed.

For this, the crew needed a plethora of instruments and equipment – thermometers, barometers, dredgers, sounding leads, huge lengths of rope. Guns were removed to make space for laboratories and extra cabins. Shelves were stacked with bottles filled with alcohol to preserve specimens.

Challenger cast off from Portsmouth on 21 December 1872, first heading south to the Canary Islands before crossing the Atlantic to the Caribbean. Over the course of a year, it zigzagged back and forth across the ocean at different latitudes, trawling the seabed, collecting specimens, recording a wealth of marine data and carrying out depth soundings.

After the final Atlantic crossing, from the Cape of Good Hope at the tip of Africa to Tristan da Cunha in South America, the ship headed south, spotting whales and icebergs around the Antarctic Circle, but reportedly never sighting the great continent itself.

From there, *Challenger* sailed west, rounding the treacherous waters off Cape Horn, before sailing across the vast ocean, stopping at islands such as Tonga and Fiji before making it to Australia in August 1874 then on up to the northern Pacific. After another eighteen months or so sailing around the Pacific and exploring the Asian coastline, the ship headed back to Europe.

One of the expedition's most impressive achievements may have been its relatively accurate measurement of the deepest area of the oceans – part of the cavernous Mariana Trench, which became known as Challenger Deep, named after the vessel.

On its 130,000-kilometre journey, the ship's crew took almost 500 deep-sea soundings, dredged the seabed over 130 times, trawled open water 150 times and took numerous other measurements, as well as collecting around 4,700 marine species new to science. Their notes filled a 50-volume, 29,500-page report, packed with illustrations and photos (new at the time). Maybe unsurprisingly, the report took a couple of decades to compile.

The success of the 1,000-day voyage is evident in its legacy, with subsequent expeditions, such as that of the *Glomar Challenger* (see page 134) and the Space Shuttle *Challenger* (see page 187) being named after it. No wonder the expedition was described by naturalist John Murray as 'the greatest advance in the knowledge of our planet since the celebrated discoveries of the fifteenth and sixteenth centuries'.

PLASTIC PLANET

The three bear cubs trail their mother from clam-hole to clam-hole. She stops to dig, and the cubs take this chance to lie down on the dark, muddy sand. Some of the group venture closer, using as cover the long grass further up the beach. The mother spots them and ambles towards the group. As she draws near, they can see the deep pile of her fur, the flies buzzing around her face. The mother loses interest and starts to munch on some grass before eventually turning her back and sauntering off. The cubs follow her over the bank, across the meadow, until they vanish from sight.

Relieved yet elated by the experience, the group return to their dingy and head on to the next beach, where they get to work scanning it for human-made debris. On this remote stretch of coast, it's incredible what they find – everything from old detergent bottles to fishing nets to oil drums. They strip the beach until it's nude again. Then they hop back on the dingy and return to the ship ready to set off for the next area of littered coastline.

This was in June 2013. On board the ship were scientists and artists, all part of Expedition GYRE – a voyage of 730 kilometres down the coast of the Gulf of Alaska with the aim of collecting and studying marine debris.

The expedition was so named because marine debris can be driven to remote, pristine parts of the world by ocean gyres – large systems of circular ocean currents formed by global wind patterns and forces created by Earth's rotation.

Much of the rubbish collected on the expedition was plastic. We now live in a plastic age. Scientists fear that one day when our descendants look back at the geological record they won't find a layer of fossils of a particular species or trinkets made of iron or bronze, but instead a film of plastic.

The facts are alarming. Experts estimate that at least 8 million tonnes of plastic is dumped in the world's oceans every year. A plastic bag was recently seen floating in the depths of the Mariana Trench (the deepest natural trench in the world, located in the western Pacific – see page 138). A trillion pieces of plastic are thought to be locked inside Arctic sea ice. A vast swirling mass of plastic, covering an area of 1.6 million square kilometres, swirls in the middle of the Pacific – dubbed the Great Pacific Garbage Patch.

While now-famous images of a turtle with a plastic straw up its nose, or a baby sperm whale with a plastic bucket lodged in its mouth, highlight how wildlife suffer from all this plastic pollution, it's the small stuff that could be even more harmful. Studies have shown that microplastics (less than 5 millimetres in size) are lining the guts of marine species. As these tiny particles make their way up the food chain, no one really knows their effect on the human body. All we do know is that they exist in the food we eat and water we drink.

The Expedition GYRE team found plenty of plastic items and also the most bizarre of debris – airplane wings, signposts from Japan (probably washed out to sea during the 2011 tsunami) and rubbish from America, such as shotgun shells and cigarette lighters.

With many of the items, the artists on board the ship created art installations, which were shown at a museum exhibition in Anchorage – a small yet vital attempt to illustrate the huge scale of the problem with our increasingly plastic planet.

HUNTING FOR THE LOCH NESS MONSTER

It had all the hallmarks of a great expedition. An international group of scientists, nicknamed the Super Natural History team, who were going to hunt for a monster. Not just any monster, but the infamous Loch Ness Monster – aka Nessie.

This enigmatic beast is the stuff of legends. Over the decades, there have been numerous supposed sightings. Blurry, unconvincing photos and films have surfaced, but all have been ridiculed as fakes or hoaxes – or simply the hallucinations of wild imaginations keen to believe the unbelievable, conjuring up images of Nessie from large branches, swimming deer, seals, boat wakes and waves. Many a Loch Ness visitor is so keen to see a huge, water-dwelling monster that in their own mind they may really see one.

Admittedly, there could be plenty of places for Nessie to hide in the vast, deep lake. At 227 metres from the surface to the deepest spot on the lake floor, London's 180-metre-high Gherkin building would be well submerged. Plus, the loch holds more water than all the lakes in England and Wales combined, and there is zero visibility below 9 metres.

Cryptozoologists, who like to believe in the existence of mythical animals from folklore, claim that Nessie could be a plesiosaur – a marine reptile with a long neck that existed during the days of the dinosaurs. And yet the odds are heavily stacked against such a theory.

Fossil evidence implies that plesiosaurs died out in a mass extinction when an asteroid struck Earth 66 million years ago. Anyway, fish populations in the lake suggest there wouldn't be enough food to sustain a 900-kilogram plesiosaur. Plus, no biological evidence (such as droppings, bones or carcasses of prey) for a huge beast has ever been recovered; divers and motion-detection cameras have never spotted anything; and vessels using sonar have never yielded any results. The case for the existence of Nessie seems well and truly closed.

So why were the Super Natural History team even bothering to hunt for Nessie? Because they wanted to try using the relatively new technique of environmental DNA (eDNA) sampling to get a definitive answer as to whether such a beast could ever have existed in the lake. The technique involves testing samples of water, sediment, air, soil or even ice for genetic traces of species. This is a bit like how a forensic scientist looks for traces of DNA at a crime scene.

What is eDNA?

Deoxyribonucleic acid (DNA) is made up of two long chains of molecules forming a spiral, like a twisted ladder – the double helix. It contains genetic information with instructions for a living organism to grow, function and reproduce. Each organism's DNA is unique. A tiny amount extracted from, say, one skin cell is enough to reveal the identity of the organism.

Back in the 1990s, scientists realized that an organism inhabiting a certain environment wouldn't need to be present all the time for them to know it lived there, as the organism would leave traces of its existence, such as flaked-off skin cells or faeces. So, by collecting so-called environmental DNA (eDNA) in water or soil samples, they would be able to determine what species lived in that habitat. Conventional wildlife surveys involve the time-consuming technique of patiently counting numbers sighted within a certain area, or setting up camera traps or submerging filming equipment in the hope that an animal will pass by. But with eDNA all you need is a trowel to dig up soil or a bucket to scoop up water and then it's back to the lab to analyse the contents.

Environmental DNA has mostly been used to gauge population sizes of known species, from newts to sharks. But geneticist Professor Neil Gemmell, from the University of Otago in New Zealand, decided to try it out on Loch Ness – partly for the fun of it and partly to gain a deeper insight into the loch's ecology. The hope was that the team might discover types of fish, molluscs or other marine species not previously known to live there and, crucially, spot any invasive species that had moved in to compete with the natives.

After lengthy journeys from various parts of the globe to the shores of Loch Ness, in May 2018 Gemmell and his international team got to work collecting water samples from the lake.

A month later, after numerous boat trips collecting many litres of water, the team packed up and headed back to the lab, where they spent months extracting DNA, sequencing genes and sifting through DNA databases to identify species living in the loch.

The expedition unearthed some interesting findings, but no sign of Nessie or the usual suspects – catfish, sturgeon or sharks. The team did find a lot of eel DNA, so the most likely culprits could be migrating giant eels.

SEARCHING FOR THE WRECK OF *ENDURANCE*

The noise on deck is deafening – a howling wind punctured by the sea splashing against the hull and the odd crack as the bow slices into another metre-thick chunk of ice. SA *Agulhas II* is getting closer to its target – 68°39'30.0' S and 52°26'30.0' W – the precise co-ordinates where Ernest Shackleton's ill-fated ship the *Endurance* sank in the Weddell Sea off Antarctica.

On 10 February 2019, the voice of ice pilot Freddie Ligthelm echoes over the tannoy: 'Good morning from the bridge. This is to say we have reached the *Endurance* sinking position. *Lekker, lekker, lekker.*' ('Nice, nice, nice' in Afrikaans.)

The wind has dropped a bit. It's cloudy, but the visibility is good. The team lower the large orange hulk of the autonomous underwater vehicle (AUV) over the side of the ship, ready to start its search for the *Endurance*. But thirty hours later the search is halted. Conditions have worsened and the AUV has become trapped under the ice. With fears that the ship might become trapped as well, the mission has to be abandoned.

As the expedition's director of exploration, Mensun Bound, said: 'Like Shackleton before us, who described the graveyard of *Endurance* as "the worst portion of the worst sea in the world", our well-laid plans were overcome by the rapidly moving ice, and what Shackleton called "the evil conditions of the Weddell Sea".'

The aim of the expedition wasn't just to search for the *Endurance*, but also to study the broken Larsen C ice shelf and the environment around it. Owned by the South African government's Department of Environmental Affairs, the 134-metre-long SA *Agulhas II* is one of the biggest and most modern polar research vessels in the world. On board are all sorts of devices: aerial drones sporting HD video and digital cameras for conservation surveillance and, alongside satellite remote sensors, to help steer the easiest route through the ice; AUVs capable of speeds of up to six knots and plunging to depths of 6,000 metres, to scan and photograph the seafloor, and measure the sea depth under the ice shelves; remotely operated vehicles (ROVs) to collect samples of flora and fauna from the seabed; and sediment corers to gather sediment samples, which provide long-term records of environmental change.

Recently, global warming has been blamed for the thinning and collapse of parts of the Larsen C ice shelf. At 44,000 square kilometres, it's the fourth-largest ice shelf in Antarctica. Back in 1995,

A tale of endurance

Built in Sandefjord in Norway in 1912, the *Endurance* set sail from Plymouth in August 1914 on what was to be her final expedition. After crossing the Atlantic, from Buenos Aires she headed for South Georgia and then on to the Weddell Sea in Antarctica. The expedition aim was to make the first land crossing of the Antarctic continent. But in January 1915 the ship became trapped in the ice. Through the Antarctic winter, the crew remained with the ship. But eventually the pressure of the ice became too much and it pierced through the hull. The time had come to abandon the ailing vessel.

Shackleton and his twenty-seven crew headed north in lifeboats. Eventually they made it to Elephant Island at the northernmost tip of Antarctica. Weakened by the challenging journey, many of the crew hunkered down, subsisting on penguins and seals. The few with any strength left joined Shackleton as he struck out for South Georgia, over 1,200 kilometres away. Incredibly, they made it. Yet they still had to scale a mountain range to reach a whaling station on the other side. After three unsuccessful attempts, Shackleton eventually reached Elephant Island to rescue the remaining crew. Everyone survived – a testament to Shackleton's tenacity.

the Larsen A ice shelf collapsed over the course of just a few weeks, then Larsen B followed suite in 2002. And, more recently, in 2017, a huge iceberg calved off the Larsen C section. As ice shelves float, they don't directly affect sea levels if they collapse, but they do act as a sort of buttress for glaciers on land that feed into them. If the Larsen C ice shelf disappears, the glaciers draining into it contain enough frozen water to raise global sea levels by about 10 centimetres.

The team are still analysing the results from the expedition, but facts like these help to highlight the crucial work of polar missions.

LOCKED IN ARCTIC ICE

Being stuck in the Arctic ice for a whole year might seem like a frightening prospect. But the German icebreaker RV *Polarstern* has been intentionally frozen into its icy bed in order to analyse the climate system at the pole over the course of a year, to help in humanity's battle against climate change.

The urgent need for such an expedition is apparent with the evidence of global warming all around us – from bleached corals in the tropics to retreating glaciers in the mountains. The Arctic is the perfect place to study the effects of climate change, as it is closely linked to weather patterns around the world and no other region has warmed as quickly over the last few decades. Indeed, at the beginning of 2018 it was warmer in the central Arctic than it was in some parts of Germany.

Yet so little is known about the central Arctic, because it is virtually inaccessible during the long polar winter. It's so far north that there are almost no polar lights and the winter ice is too thick for even the toughest of icebreakers to penetrate.

The only way to access this central region was to intentionally lock a ship into drifting ice. So, in autumn 2019, the *Polarstern* crew cast off from Tromsø in Norway, bound for the Siberian sea ice and on the hunt for a large ice floe – it needed to be several kilometres in diameter and at least 1.5 metres thick. They found a suitable one to anchor on to; then, as the winter progressed, the ice around the ship thickened, dragging it along at a rate of around 7 kilometres a day.

This isn't the first time that a boat has been intentionally frozen into the ice. Zoologist and explorer Fridtjof Nansen – known as 'the father of polar exploration' – did just this back in 1893, surviving to tell the tale (see page 46). But never before has an Arctic expedition been undertaken on such a grand scale. In total, 60 institutes from 17 countries, made up of 600 experts and 300 support personnel, are involved in the €120 million project, known as the Multidisciplinary drifting Observatory for the Study of Arctic Climate (MOSAiC).

Over the course of the year, the experts will rotate on and off the ship, working on different science experiments both on board the *Polarstern* and at different bases set up on the ice, some up to 50 kilometres away from the vessel.

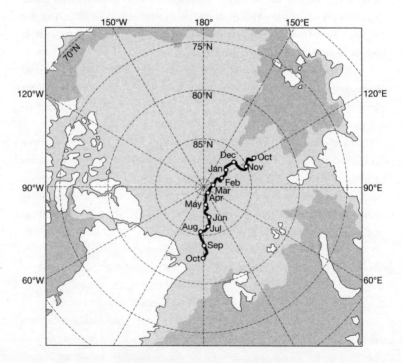

The *Polarstern*'s expected drift route

The aim is to study how polar clouds, ocean dynamics and ice formation all contribute to the worrying shift we've seen in recent years of ice-free summers in the Arctic. By moving with the natural 'transpolar drift', the team will gain first-hand insight into the annual sea-ice cycle as it evolves from new first-year ice to multi-year ice and then how it breaks up as it approaches the North Atlantic.

The logistics behind such an ambitious expedition are challenging. The *Polarstern* is being accompanied by four icebreakers at different times throughout the course of the journey, as well as three research aircraft providing support and supplies. It's the first time that planes have been used for extended flights in the central Arctic. But fuel depots have been set up to ensure that team members can be evacuated immediately by helicopter if needed.

All sorts of hi-tech equipment is required – from scientific instruments to carry out the experiments through to heavy-duty kit like snowcats and ice cutters to carve out landing strips for the planes.

The *Polarstern* is due to be released from the Arctic's icy grip in autumn 2020, when it reaches the Fram Strait between Greenland and Svalbard. The 2,500-kilometre journey will revolutionize our understanding of Arctic science. As the project's chief scientist, Professor Markus Rex, says, 'This will take us to areas that are beyond anything we can imagine.'

PART 3

OCEAN DEPTHS

While we know a fair amount about the shallow seas, far less is known about the ocean depths. Throughout history, only a brave few have ventured into the gloomy aquatic underworld of bizarre deep-sea monsters. In 1934, the steel ball of the bathysphere plunged to 923 metres below the sea surface. Then in 1960, the Trieste submersible dived 11 kilometres down to the deepest part of the ocean, Challenger Deep. These and similar expeditions smashed previous world records and brought incredible insight into marine life deep beneath the waves.

THE BATHYSPHERE

'There is one joy of reading, another of painting, and another of writing, but none to compare with the thrill which comes to one who, loving Nature in all her moods, is about to start on a voyage of discovery to a land familiar in dreams alone.' These were the words of naturalist William Beebe. It was 1934 and, alongside Otis Barton, he was about to make the deepest ocean dive in history.

Their vessel was a steel ball, 1.4 metres wide and weighing 2 tonnes, which its designer Barton called the bathysphere: 'bathus' meaning 'deep', so 'deep sphere'. Barton opted for the spherical design, as that was the best shape to withstand the extreme pressures of the deep ocean. (For every 10 metres deeper, the pressure increases by about one atmosphere.) The bathysphere had walls 3.8 centimetres thick and three portholes, 7.5 centimetres thick, were made from fused quartz – a tough material for the time, which transmitted light well in the ocean depths. Stashed inside the vessel were two oxygen tanks, and pans of calcium carbonate to soak up moisture and soda lime to absorb exhaled carbon dioxide. The bathysphere was unpowered and so had to be winched down and up through the water via a cable attached to a boat on the surface.

Otis Barton was a wealthy inventor, born in New York in 1899, while Charles William Beebe was a naturalist and director of the New York Zoological Society's Department of Tropical Research. Born in New York in 1877, his fascination with the natural world developed when the family moved to New Jersey. While many teenagers would have been experimenting with relationships and mind-altering substances, Beebe started collecting specimens for taxidermy. And while still at high school he wrote his first article on the brown creeper bird. Always adventurous, at university he convinced his professors to sponsor him and a few other students to go on a research expedition to Nova Scotia. Many adventures followed, but his deep-sea expedition with Barton was to make him famous.

It was 15 August 1934. One by one, the two men, both about 1.8 metres tall, clambered into the cramped bathysphere. This wasn't the first time the pair had plunged into the ocean depths, but it would be the first time anyone had ever gone so deep.

Metre by metre the bathysphere descended through the waters off Nonsuch Island in Bermuda. At 923 metres below the surface, it ran out of the cable that attached it to the support boat on the surface. The vessel could go no deeper.

As the men peered out of the portholes, many of the creatures they saw were new to science – or were unrecognizable compared to the dead, bloated versions previously hauled to the surface. And never before had the behaviour of these deep-sea beasts been observed in their natural environment. Beebe and Barton marvelled at bizarre-looking creatures such as the school of luminous pale green jellyfish, the crafty angler fish that lured unwitting prey into its jaws with a fleshy growth protruding from its head, or the jawless lamprey eel: 'If tentacles were needed by this eel why in the name of holy natural selection must the jaws be thus sacrificed!' said Beebe. 'How they live and move and satisfy their appetites in the icy blackness half a mile beneath our keel I shall perhaps never know.'

But the men were given only a few minutes at maximum depth before the bathysphere started to be winched up again. Beebe had wanted to spend longer down there, but it was deemed too dangerous. The men returned safely to the surface, having smashed the previous deepest dive world record of just over 100 metres.

Beebe and Barton with their invention

More deep-sea adventures followed for the pair. Observations from each dive were carefully noted by a team of scientists at the surface, listening to Beebe's vivid descriptions of the incredible array of deep-sea life, which he relayed via a radio hooked up to the cable.

All the bizarre creatures encountered on the expedition went on to feature in Beebe's subsequent bestselling book *Half Mile Down*. So, not only did the expedition give an insight into this previously unknown dark, alien world, but it was also – considering the technology of the time – a truly courageous feat and a milestone in oceanographic exploration. As Beebe put it: 'The supreme joy of learning, of discovering, of adding our tiny facts to the foundation of the everlasting why of the universe; all this makes life one never-ending delight.'

TECTONIC DISCOVERY

It was August 1955, the *Pioneer*, had been commissioned by the US Navy and the Scripps Institution of Oceanography to conduct a detailed survey of the seafloor off the Washington-Oregon coast. It was the first time that a marine magnetometer had been used to measure the magnetism of the seafloor. Yet it would prove to be a groundbreaking voyage for science. As one eminent geologist described it: 'One of the most significant geophysical surveys ever made.' And a major step in the formation of the theory of plate tectonics.

Back in the early 1900s, geologist Alfred Wegener had come up with the theory of continental drift, claiming that the continents had once formed a single landmass, before breaking apart and drifting to their present locations (see page 50). He'd recognized that the continents of the world fitted together like a jigsaw puzzle, which would explain why rock strata in South Africa and Brazil were identical while fern fossils from tropical climes matched those found in the Arctic. But he didn't know exactly how the continents had drifted.

Initially, Wegener was ridiculed for this idea. Over the years, his theory of continental drift gradually gained traction in academic circles; yet still no one understood the mechanism of how the continents could move.

Harry Hess was a professor of geology at Princeton University. During the Second World War, as an officer in the navy, he made

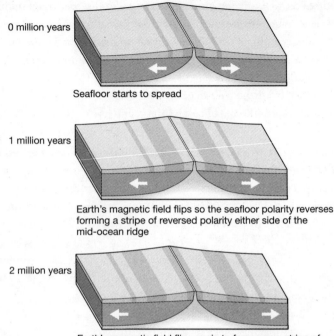

0 million years

Seafloor starts to spread

1 million years

Earth's magnetic field flips so the seafloor polarity reverses forming a stripe of reversed polarity either side of the mid-ocean ridge

2 million years

Earth's magnetic field flips again to form a new stripe of normal polarity either side of the mid-ocean ridge

How seafloor spreading works

an astounding discovery. While sailing across the North Pacific, he used sonar to map the seafloor. His results showed that it was even more irregular than imagined – full of huge deep trenches and great volcanic sea mountains.

Hess noticed that the deepest parts of the oceans were at the edges of the continents, while the shallower areas were in the middle, which seemed to suggest that oceans grew from their centres. Hess thought it could be because the seafloor tore apart, creating cracks for magma to spill out of on to the seafloor, building new crust, which over time spread away from the mid-ocean ridge.

Results from the 1955 *Pioneer* voyage helped support his theory. The survey had discovered a pattern of long, linear magnetic stripes on the seafloor, from which geologists were able to work out its age. The further from the mid-ocean ridge, the older the crust, which confirmed Hess's theory of seafloor spreading.

Ageing the seafloor

Earth's crust is made up of a jigsaw of tectonic plates, which float on a fluid layer called the 'asthenosphere', driven by hot, convective currents deep within the mantle. Where the plates diverge and oceanic crust is ripped apart, rising hot magma spills out on to the seafloor at what's known as a mid-ocean ridge. This process of 'seafloor spreading' continues as the plates pull apart. Before the cooling magma hardens on the seafloor, it becomes magnetized in the direction of Earth's magnetic field. This is because iron-rich crystals in the magma align with the Earth's magnetic field, a bit like a compass needle is pulled towards magnetic north.

Every so often the planet's magnetic field reverses. This has happened hundreds of times over the last few billion years. However, on average, it's been every 200,000 to 300,000 years in the last 20 million years – although twice that long since the last time it flipped.

A device known as a magnetometer can be used to measure the direction of magnetism, which forms a symmetrical pattern of stripes of normal polarity and reversed polarity on the seafloor either side of a mid-ocean ridge. This pattern of stripes reveals the rate of so-called 'seafloor spreading' – the broader the stripe, the faster the spreading rate – helping to age the seafloor.

More evidence was gathered in the 1970s when the ship *Glomar Challenger* was sent on a fifteen-year expedition, known as the Deep Sea Drilling Program. Capable of drilling to more than 1,700 metres, the vessel zigzagged back and forth between Africa and South America, across the Mid-Atlantic Ridge, investigating over 600 sites on the seafloor. Its results showed that the seafloor was older at drill sites further away from the mid-ocean ridge, providing more concrete evidence for seafloor spreading.

And this, in turn, led to the development of the theory of plate tectonics – whereby the planet's outer shell is divided into several plates that glide over the mantle – which is now a staple of geology textbooks around the world.

DIVING UNDER THE NORTH POLE

The voice of Commander William R. Anderson echoes through the submarine: 'In a few moments we will realize a goal, long a dream of mankind, the attainment by ship of the geographic North Pole. Stand by … 10, 8, 6, 5, 4, 3, 2, 1 … For the USA and the US Navy. Sunday 3 August 1958; 2315 Eastern Daylight Saving Time. The North Pole.' A huge cheer rings out among the other 115 men on board. The world's first nuclear-powered submarine has just made the first-ever voyage under the Arctic ice cap.

Named after Jules Verne's fictional submarine in *Twenty Thousand Leagues Under the Sea*, the *Nautilus* was an engineering marvel for its time – a uranium-powered nuclear reactor created steam that drove turbines, propelling the sub underwater at speeds of up to twenty knots.

The diesel-electric submarines that existed before the *Nautilus* could dive for only a limited amount of time, surfacing regularly to recharge their batteries. But this nuclear-powered sub had an almost limitless range, meaning it could remain underwater for weeks instead of hours, surfacing only occasionally. Ideal for military warfare if things got a bit heated with the Soviets.

Construction on the submarine had begun in 1951, under the meticulous eye of navy engineer Captain Hyman G. Rickover, who was born in Russia but joined the US atomic programme in 1946. Recognizing that this project was of huge national importance, Rickover pushed his team to build the submarine in record time. He reputedly once said about a tiny hole discovered in the hull, which was a third of the width of a human hair: 'Small leaks usually seal themselves.' Rather than just hoping it would, one of the team suggested buying some radiator 'stop leak' to put in the seawater inside the condenser. Problem solved.

As the project developed, it became ever more important to the national interest: the submarine's keel was laid by President Harry Truman in 1952, while First Lady Mamie Eisenhower broke a bottle of champagne on its bow before its maiden voyage up the Thames River in Connecticut on 21 January 1954. By 1957,

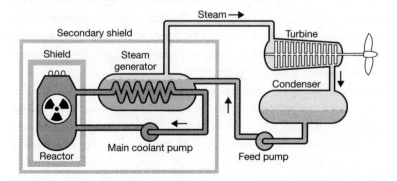

A nuclear reactor on a submarine

the *Nautilus* was ready for its greatest test – to try to reach the North Pole.

The first attempt in August ended badly: the navigational equipment failed and the submarine had to turn back. But the pressure was on to try again as, in October of that year, the Soviet Union took the lead in the battle for technological supremacy with the successful launch of *Sputnik 1* (see page 170). The US needed to show it wasn't falling behind.

A second attempt was made in April 1958, but the *Nautilus* could not find a safe route through the Chukchi Sea, as ice floes ranged in depth from 15 to 50 metres. Another failure. A new plan was needed.

Over the next few months, navigational recces were conducted with flights over the ice cap, while Alaskan fishermen were quizzed about the best fishing grounds, giving an idea of the best route through the ice. The submarine was ready to try again.

Casting off from Point Barrow in Alaska on 1 August 1958, the *Nautilus* navigated its way through the ice floe maze of the Chukchi Sea. Two days later, the sub passed under the North Pole.

The crew had to wait two days until the ice cleared and they could resurface in the Greenland Sea, before being able to relay the news to Washington via Morse code. To capitalize on the endeavour, Captain Anderson was picked up from the submarine and flown by helicopter to the capital to be paraded in front of the world's media. 'I'm a little bit dazed right now. Fourteen hours ago I was submerged. Seventy-two hours under ice. And only five days ago at the North Pole.'

Meanwhile, the *Nautilus* headed to Iceland and then steamed on to the Isle of Portland on the south coast of Britain. From where it had initially cast off in Hawaii, it had covered more than 13,000 kilometres, 96 per cent of which had been underwater.

How a nuclear sub works

The nuclear reactor sits inside a thick metal casing made from a special alloy, which provides protection from the radioactive fuel rods. A reactor essentially works like a steam engine. Inside the reactor, a neutron splits an atom of uranium, generating energy as gamma radiation and heat. As water passes through a coil next to the reactor, it becomes very hot – but doesn't boil, because it is forced through under high pressure. The water is then pumped through a steam generator and back into the reactor for reheating. Meanwhile, in a secondary system, the steam drives turbine generators that supply the ship with electricity, as well as the main turbines, which drive the propeller. As no oxygen is needed for this process, the submarine doesn't need to surface for air.

Never before had such a voyage been undertaken. The *Nautilus* was a huge milestone in nuclear and submarine engineering. And the mission had been a success on many levels. The crew had shown great courage – if anything had gone wrong under the ice, no other vessel would have been able to rescue the sub. Commander Anderson received the prestigious Legion of Merit from President Dwight D. Eisenhower, while the crew received a Presidential Unit Citation and were given a hero's welcome on their return to New York. Plus, the *Nautilus* kick-started a new military era – the limitless range of nuclear submarines changed naval strategy and tactics for ever.

INTO THE ABYSS

The submarine's floodlights illuminate the darkness, picking out a few jellyfish, some shrimp-like creatures and a white flatfish, around 30 centimetres long, shuffling on the seafloor. Its eyes shift to look at the vessel, the first time light has ever bathed its inky world. Jacques Piccard turns to Don Walsh and shakes his hand. At almost 11 kilometres beneath the sea surface, the men have just made history – diving to the deepest known place in the world's oceans, Challenger Deep.

Named after the ship HMS *Challenger*, which carried out the first survey of its depths back in 1875 (see page 114), Challenger Deep is a slot-shaped trough at the bottom of a much larger depression – the Mariana Trench, around 300 kilometres south-west of the Pacific island of Guam.

It was 23 January 1960. The men were tucked inside the relative safety of the *Trieste* – an Italian-built submersible, named after the town where much of it was built and designed by Jacques Piccard's father, Swiss inventor Auguste Piccard. Alongside Jacques was Don Walsh, a lieutenant in the US Navy, who famously once said: 'More people have walked on the moon than have been to the deepest place in the ocean.'

While the *Trieste* was 18 metres long, the cabin attached to the belly of the steel submersible was only about 2 metres wide. Much of the rest of the vessel was taken up by 9 tonnes of iron pellets to weigh it down and over 126,000 litres of gasoline for buoyancy. A steel wall of 12.7 centimetres protected them from the immense external pressure (about 8 tonnes per square inch), and they peered out through a cone of clear acrylic at the alien world outside. The descent took four hours and forty-eight minutes, diving at a rate of around a metre a second.

The Mariana Trench

At 2,542 kilometres long, and 10.9 kilometres deep at the bottom of Challenger Deep, the Mariana Trench is five times the length of the Grand Canyon and more than 2 kilometres deeper under the sea surface than Mount Everest is high. At these depths, the pressure is 1,000 times that at sea level. And yet life has evolved to deal with such extreme pressures. The Mariana Trench is home to some truly bizarre creatures, such as the dumbo octopus (which swallows its prey whole), the deep-sea dragonfish, the pink-coloured goblin shark and zombie worms. The vast trench exists because it sits at a subduction zone, where one huge slab of oceanic crust is being forced down below another.

The closest land is US territory Guam and the Mariana Islands, which make up a commonwealth of the US. In 2009, President George W. Bush made the Mariana Trench into a Marine National Monument. Creating this protected marine environment could be vital if one day more marine explorers venture into its depths.

All was going well until, suddenly, a loud crack rang ominously through the craft, followed by juddering. The men scrambled to identify the cause of the noise, realizing that if the vessel was breached at this depth of 9,000 metres the pressure outside would soon turn them to pulp. But their instruments were functioning normally, indicating that it couldn't be too serious. Once near the seafloor they hunted for the cause – a cracked acrylic window on the entrance tunnel. Nothing could be done about it.

The pair explained this to the support ship on the surface via a hydrophone system, waiting seven seconds for their message to get through. Then they spent the rest of the twenty minutes at that depth, observing their surroundings and eating their way through some chocolate bars – to keep their energy up in the chilly cabin, where temperatures were just 7 degrees Celsius. After ditching the ballast, the submersible started to rise back up to civilization – taking three hours and fifteen minutes to reach the surface.

No manned vessel had ever ventured deeper in the oceans and, although robots have gone back, only one other person has dived so deep again – director James Cameron, famous for his films *Titanic* and *Avatar*, who made a solo descent in 2012. While Cameron's subsequent films gave a whole new insight into life at such depths, it was the observations by Piccard and Walsh that changed the dogma at the time that no life could exist so deep. And the two men deserve a pat on the back for taking on the challenge, which could so easily have ended in disaster. Yet maybe the greatest accolade should go to Auguste Piccard for designing such an engineering marvel – a milestone in oceanographic exploration.

RIDING THE GULF STREAM

The year 1969 will forever be etched in our memories as the year that humans first stepped on to the moon. And yet, while the eyes of the world were trained on *Apollo 11*, a different NASA mission was happening in another unexplored world – the deep ocean.

A 15m-long submarine called the *Ben Franklin* was drifting with the Gulf Stream up the east coast of the United States, gathering scientific data. This mission was equally daring, equally technically challenging, equally invaluable to science. And yet, after thirty-one days floating in the ocean depths, the six-man crew on board the

Ben Franklin surfaced to no fanfare, no TV crews, no presidential congratulations. Their courageous expedition had been totally eclipsed by the moon landing.

While the Gulf Stream expedition has been all but forgotten in the annals of history, there were a number of parallels between it and *Apollo 11*. Both were NASA missions, launched from the east coast of Florida, venturing into the unknown – one travelling through the darkness of space, in contact with mission control in Houston and exploring the rugged lunar terrain; the other travelling through the darkness of the ocean depths, in contact with the escort ship *Privateer* and exploring the seafloor's rugged terrain. Both the *Ben Franklin* submarine and the *Apollo 11* lunar module were built by Grumman Corporation. Both missions were incredibly risky – if anything went wrong, there would be little hope of recovery. And both space and marine exploration had been declared key national goals by President John F. Kennedy back in 1961: he stated that 'We choose to go to the moon in this decade ...'; and that '... a national effort in the basic and applied research of oceanography ... Knowledge of the oceans is more than a matter of curiosity. Our very survival may hinge upon it.'

The missions weren't supposed to coincide. The best window of opportunity to launch the Gulf Stream mission was in May. Yet technical issues kept the submarine moored at the dock in Palm Beach, Florida, for a number of weeks. It eventually cast off on 14 July 1969, just two days before the *Apollo 11* launch.

The mission leader was Swiss oceanographer and engineer Jacques Piccard who, along with Don Walsh, was already famous for reaching the bottom of Challenger Deep in 1960 (see page 138). The rest of the crew was made up of a navy captain, an engineer, an acoustic specialist, an oceanographer and a NASA scientist, whose job it was to observe the social dynamics on board to gain an insight into the effect that prolonged isolation would have on humans in space.

The Gulf Stream

The Gulf Stream is a warm, swift current that runs from Florida up the east coast of the US and Canada before crossing the Atlantic to Europe. Without the Gulf Stream, the climate in Western Europe would be a lot chillier. It exists because of differences in temperature and salt content. When warm water from the equator flows north to cooler climes, freshwater evaporates causing the sea to become saltier, making it denser, so it sinks down to the level of deep ocean currents.

The Gulf Stream is part of a much larger global system called the Thermohaline Circulation or Meridional Overturning Circulation. After travelling through the world's deep ocean basins, the dense water will rise back up to the surface in a process known as 'upwelling'.

One by one, early on the morning of 14 July, the crew entered the submarine that would be their home for thirty-one days. The *Privateer* slowly towed the sub out to sea, then at 10.30 p.m. the last hatch was closed, the ballast tanks flooded and the *Ben Franklin* sank beneath the waves.

At first everything appeared to be all right. But as the submarine descended ever deeper, the crew started to notice small leaks springing up. Some fuses blew, the temperature dropped to below 12 degrees Celsius and communication was lost with the *Privateer*. It was a worrying time for the crew. But, eventually, they managed to rectify the issues – breathing a collective sigh of relief.

By 20 July, while the *Apollo 11* astronauts were taking giant leaps for mankind and planting the US flag, the *Ben Franklin* aquanauts had been busy at work for a number of days – measuring water temperature and salinity, observing marine life, carrying out acoustic

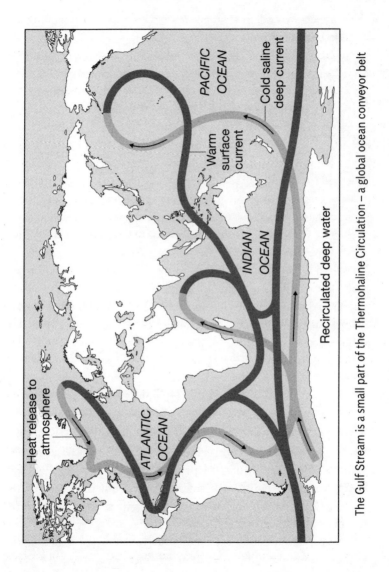

The Gulf Stream is a small part of the Thermohaline Circulation – a global ocean conveyor belt

experiments, recording magnetic anomalies and photographing and mapping the seafloor.

In any downtime, the crew ate freeze-dried rations, played Scrabble, poker and darts, and read or listened to music – 'On the Road Again' by Willy Nelson became a firm crew favourite.

Over the course of the voyage there were more dramas. At one point the submarine got caught in a huge eddy and was fired out of the Gulf Stream. After attempting to use energy-hungry engines to rejoin the main current, the crew gave up and surfaced to hitch a lift with the *Privateer* – although the hatches remained sealed, despite soaring temperatures and 100 per cent humidity.

Finally, on 14 August, three weeks after *Apollo 11* splashed down in the Pacific, the *Ben Franklin* resurfaced off the coast of Nova Scotia. The crew opened a hatch for the first time in thirty-one days. They had not only survived a challenging mission, drifting for over 2,600 kilometres in the ocean depths, but also amassed a wealth of scientific data about the Gulf Stream and the submarine world that it flows through. The result: a detailed insight into the current that influences our climate.

FINDING THE TITANIC

A purple octopus scavenges over a mound of giant clams, each one the size of a watermelon. Crabs scuttle past. A pink fish brushes through red-tipped tubeworms that cling to a rocky tower. A cloud of black escapes from the peak of the tower, like a smoking chimney. Intrigued, the submersible circles back for a better look.

On the surface, 2.5 kilometres above, oceanographer Robert Ballard is taking notes aboard the launch ship RV *Lulu*, jotting down the words of submersible pilot Jack Corliss as he describes the seascape before him. 'Isn't the deep ocean supposed to be like a desert?' asks Corliss. 'Well, there's all these animals down here.'

This was dive number 713 for submersible *Alvin*, and yet it was the first time that anyone had plunged to the depths of the Galapagos Rift – a spur of the mid-ocean ridge in the Pacific Ocean, which is the largest submarine mountain range in the world. Following this expedition in 1977, this remote spot became known as the site of one of the most important discoveries ever made in ocean science.

When the seafloor is torn apart due to 'seafloor spreading' (see page 131), rising magma escapes through so-called 'hydrothermal vents'. When the magma hits freezing seawater it forms a black cloud, as seen by the submersible team. Some of the particles in the cloud settle, eventually building up to form the chimney-like shapes. The seawater around these 'black smokers' can reach temperatures of 300 degrees Celsius – warming the freezing seawater to create a balmy environment for marine creatures close by.

As specimens are hauled up to the surface, they are taken to the small lab in the bowels of the ship *Lulu*. Some are stashed away in the limited formaldehyde on board, others simply put in some strong Russian vodka bought in Panama. When that runs out, the specimens are just left in the open air.

Later, when the team examine these specimens, it dawns on them how life could exist so far down in the depths of the ocean. The smell of rotten eggs begins to fill the lab. Portholes are flung open. That smell could mean only one thing – hydrogen sulphide. The presence of this stinky gas means that certain minerals must be spewing out of the hydrothermal vents. The team realize that microbes could harvest chemical energy from these minerals, in a process known as chemosynthesis. Other creatures can then feed on the microbes, which explains how such a thriving community can survive at such depth, far from any light for photosynthesis. Subsequent dives in the submersible *Alvin* on the same expedition reveal the rich diversity of life clustered around other hydrothermal vents.

This discovery of vibrant communities living around hydrothermal vents radically changed the perception at that time that the deep ocean is just a vast desert. And it gave rise to the idea that the very first life forms may have evolved around hydrothermal vents, harnessing the Earth's energy as opposed to that of the sun. In interviews over the following years, Ballard said that the most fascinating thing he ever saw were the creatures living in and around deep-sea vents. And this was from the man who discovered the wreck of the *Titanic*.

Ballard famously said that he grew up wanting to be Captain Nemo from the film *20,000 Leagues Under the Sea*. He certainly got as close to that as anyone could – becoming one of the greatest marine explorers of all time.

After gaining a PhD in marine geology and geophysics, he began his career in the navy and was based for three decades at the Woods Hole Oceanographic Institution. It was while there that he managed to convince the then deputy chief of naval operations for submarine warfare to fund the development of the robotic submersible technology that he needed to find the *Titanic*. The deputy chief agreed on one condition: the prime goal of the expedition would be to search for the wrecks of the USS *Thresher* and USS *Scorpion*, in an attempt to determine two things. The first was to investigate whether the nuclear reactors that had powered the ships were causing environmental problems – if not, other nuclear material could be disposed of in the deep sea. Secondly, to determine whether foul play had sunk the ships – after all, this was the Cold War era. Only if there was any time left could Ballard take a look for the *Titanic*, which was believed to have sunk in a similar area.

During his hunt for the sunken submarines, Ballard realized that ocean currents meant that heavier material sunk quicker. And so, when he came to search for the *Titanic*, he worked off the assumption that debris might be scattered over a long range. He was right.

In September 1985, Ballard discovered the *Titanic* using powerful sonar. The grainy images of the wreck, which had lain for seventy-three years at the bottom of the ocean, 3 kilometres down, caused huge excitement when they were broadcast around the world.

Since this discovery, Ballard has discovered other wrecks, such as JFK's boat *PT-109* and the German battleship *Bismarck* sunk by the British Navy in 1941, as well as the remains of ancient ships in the Mediterranean and Black Sea.

During his lifetime, Ballard has been involved in over 120 marine expeditions and clocked more hours in the ocean depths than anyone else on the planet. His love of the deep ocean has brought its wonders to the world through the telecommunications tech he helped develop, which lets people around the globe join him on his deep-sea adventures. His numerous books and scientific papers are testament to the fact that Ballard isn't just an explorer, but also a great scientist.

OCTOGENARIAN AQUANAUT

After needing some help to get into the cumbersome body part of the suit, Sylvia Earle has the huge helmet lowered over her head and locked into place. It looks a bit like an astronaut's spacesuit, except it is made of hard plastic and metal, with multi-jointed limbs, pincer-like hands and stubby boots. The boat bobs on the waves off the coast of the Hawaiian island Oahu. But this is no holiday jaunt. Earle is about to make a historic dive to the ocean depths.

Earle was born in 1935 in New Jersey, but her interest in wildlife really developed after her family moved to Florida. It was while studying botany for her degree at Florida State University that she first tried scuba diving. In those days, there was no training, let alone a PADI course. Earle was just told to breathe naturally and down she went. This was the start of a life-long love affair with the deep.

In 1970, she was in charge of the first all-female team to live 15 metres underwater for over a week in a special submarine module known as Tektite II, stationed off the coast of St John in the US Virgin Islands. This was part psychology experiment, part marine research project, and Earle and her team split their time between the submarine module and forays into the surrounding waters to observe and record marine species. After surfacing from her stay, Earle was thrust into the media spotlight. Just a year after Armstrong and Aldrin walked on the moon, the press and public were almost as captivated by these scientists living underwater.

Then, in 1979, Earle prepared for the dive that was to make her name famous around the world. In September, Earle and her team travelled to Oahu. She hadn't previously used a Jim suit (see box). In fact, it had mostly been used in industry, rarely for science.

After donning the suit, Earle was hooked on to a flat-decked vehicle that was lowered over the side of the boat. The deck gradually sank below the waves, descending to a depth of 18 metres. Then a small submersible took over, carrying Earle the rest of the way down to the ocean floor. Once there, one of the two men inside the submersible turned a handle to release the safety belt. Shuffling forward, she stepped down on to the seafloor, 380 metres below the sea surface.

At these depths, without an atmospheric diving suit (ADS), the pressure of around 600 pounds per square inch would instantly crush the human body. But the Jim suit protected her. There was even room inside for her to remove her arms from the suit's arms in order to write in her notebook about the wonders of the deep sea world that she was experiencing. For two and a half hours, Earle explored the seafloor, moving slowly up slopes and over ridges, across a terrain that she imagined looked like the surface of the moon.

The evolution of atmospheric diving suits

When Sylvia Earle walked across the seafloor 380 metres below the surface back in 1979, the Jim suit she wore was the very latest in diving tech. Atmospheric diving suits (ADS) were first used in the early twentieth century for deep diving missions, such as salvaging wrecks. Invented in 1932 by engineer Joseph Peress, the Tritonia was the first of its kind to have flexible joints. Peress was also involved in developing the Jim suit in the 1970s. It was named after his assistant Jim Jarret, who had dived to a depth of 123 metres in Loch Ness in the Tritonia. The successor to the Jim suit is the exosuit. At 1.8 metres tall and weighing 240 kilos, with rotary joints in the limbs, thrusters in the feet, and a fibre-optic tether for two-way comms, this ADS is built for exploring marine life at extreme depths.

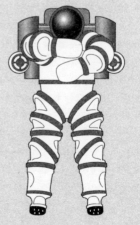

No one before (and no one since) had dived so deep without a tether to the surface. But at all times throughout the dive, Earle remained attached to the submersible by a 5-metre line. When her time was up, it was this line that dragged her back to the surface, propelled by the submersible.

The Jim suit was pressurized, so Earle didn't experience any decompression sickness – 'the bends'. Back on the boat, the helmet was lifted off her head, and she smiled, breathing the fresh sea air. It was 1979, and 'Her Deepness' (as she became known) made headlines around the world.

Now in her eighties, throughout her life Earle has been in charge of more than 100 expeditions and spent over 7,000 hours underwater – not far off a year of her life. After her walk on the seafloor, alongside engineer Graham Hawkes she started two companies that made deep-sea vehicles. Then, in the early 1990s, she became the first woman to be made Chief Scientist of the National Oceanographic and Atmospheric Administration (NOAA).

She now focuses her time on Mission Blue – the not-for-profit initiative that she started in 2009, with the aim of getting legal protection for 20 per cent of the oceans by 2020. In 2016, when President Obama announced that Hawaii's Papahānaumokuākea Marine National Monument would be expanded and made off-limits to fishing, Earle was by his side.

Over the years, Earle's love affair with the ocean has seen her do so much for marine conservation. And, despite her age, she has no plans to stop scuba diving any time soon: 'As long as I'm breathing, I'll be diving.'

THE DAY THE DINOSAURS DIED

As Dino the dinosaur looks up from his lunch, little does he know that it is going to be a bad day. Indeed, a bad day of many bad years. His eyes follow the blazing fireball as it rips through the sky. Most asteroids burn up as they pass through Earth's atmosphere, but this space rock is vast – 10 kilometres wide – speeding at 20 kilometres per second towards modern-day Yucatan, smashing into the coastline with a thunderous boom. The impact packs a punch more than 1 billion times the force of the Hiroshima bomb.

Inside the 180-kilometre-wide crater everything is instantly vaporized. Thick dust is flung into the atmosphere. Over the next few weeks, the dust envelopes the planet, blocking out the sun. It is the start of months of endless nights. With no sunlight, temperatures plummet, plants wither, and one by one the dinosaurs keel over. This event 66 million years ago was the end of their 180-million-year reign.

The dinosaurs were unlucky. If the asteroid had hit just thirty seconds later, things could have been very different. If it had plunged into the deep ocean, it would have triggered mega-tsunamis but they would not have been enough to wipe out most life.

The rocks in the area were rich in hydrocarbons and sulphur. Along with huge amounts of dust, the impact fired into the atmosphere around 325 gigatons of sulphur and 425 gigatons of carbon dioxide – more than ten times human-made carbon-dioxide emissions in 2014. Over the coming years, around 75 per cent of species died out. All that was left were a few hardy creatures – the ones that eventually gave rise to modern-day birds, reptiles and mammals. Lucky for us humans.

Various intrepid scientists have hunted for clues over the years as to how the dinosaurs died out. But, it wasn't until 1980 that father and son Luis and Walter Alvarez came up with a theory – which stuck. On a field trip in Gubbio, Italy, the pair found 66-million-year-old sedimentary rocks that contained huge concentrations of iridium – a metal not common on Earth. Meteorite showers have been found to sprinkle the planet with tiny amounts, but this layer contained ten times the normal levels. It must have arrived on a huge asteroid – and been flung into the atmosphere, settling far away from the initial impact site. Rocks in Stevns Klint in Denmark also showed an iridium spike.

But where was the impact site? In 1991, a tenacious PhD student, Alan Hildebrand, followed the treasure hunt and tracked it down. He found that the Italian and Danish rocks studied by Alvarez were thinner than ones subsequently discovered in Texas and Caribbean islands like Haiti. Hildebrand was closing in. But the Chicxulub crater eluded him for a while – partly because it was hidden under dense jungle or beneath the sea, and covered by sediment. But once Hildebrand had tracked the crater site down, he used evidence from local oil boreholes to prove it existed. The scientific establishment finally came to accept that an asteroid had killed off the dinosaurs.

More recently, an international team has dug into the heart of the Chicxulub impact crater to get more detail on the cataclysmic event. In 2014, Expedition 364 set up camp on a drilling platform, 30 kilometres off the Mexican coast. Over the course of two months they drilled ever deeper into the crater, extracting rock cores from many hundreds of metres down. The expedition wasn't without its set-backs – like the moment when a 200-metre-long piece of pipe fell into the drill hole. But, within a week, service had resumed and cores were being pulled up to the surface twenty-four-seven.

To the untrained eye, most of the cores look just like long tubes of dirt and grime. But each tells a different story. Indeed, core 40 was especially interesting because it contained rock fragments, very different in composition to the 39 cores of limestone before it. The jumbled mess of shattered and melted fragments – known as 'breccia' – was strewn across the area just minutes or hours after impact. Crucially, just above this layer were microfossils – the ghosts of creatures that either survived the event or flourished afterwards. And, within 100,000 years, dozens of different species existed. Life had returned.

MINING THE DEEP

The moon beams a light across the sea to the ship. On deck, last-minute adjustments are being made to the respiration lander – a large contraption made up of about twenty orange floats stuck on a metal ring frame. After the signal that all is ready, the device is hoisted up over the side and then released into the deep. Its mission – to bring back samples from the seafloor.

It's spring 2015. This is the second expedition of the ABYSSLINE project – an international research programme to find out what wildlife live on and under the seabed at extreme depths around what are known as 'polymetallic nodules'. Found all around the globe, these lumps of mineral deposits range in size from a pea to a football and are rich in precious metals – cobalt, copper, iron, manganese, nickel and rare-earth metals – which are used in all sorts of electronic devices from smartphones to tablets.

Having intensively mined the land for these valuable metals, in order to keep up with our thirst for new gadgets, pioneering excavators are now exploring remote parts of the ocean for potential sites with polymetallic nodules, and also underwater mountains known as seamounts, and tall chimney-like structures called hydrothermal vents.

Cold War deception

Deep-sea mining has been on the cards for decades. But it was once used as an excuse for military espionage. In the summer of 1974, a drilling ship set sail from Long Beach, California. The *Hughes Glomar Explorer* was supposed to explore the seabed for polymetallic nodules, but the voyage was actually a big cover-up for a completely different mission – finding a lost Soviet submarine.

It was the Cold War era. Six years previously, the *K-129* had sunk 2,400 kilometres off the coast of Hawaii. It had been loaded with ballistic nuclear missiles, which the Americans were keen to get their hands on to check the Soviet technology. The Russians had tried and failed to retrieve the lost sub, but the Americans worked out its location from a web of underwater listening posts. A cleverly concocted PR campaign was set in motion. Billionaire inventor Howard Hughes was enlisted to pretend to fund the expedition. While drilling equipment was visible on deck, down below, the ship had been designed with a huge claw-like device to haul the 2,000-tonne sub up from its watery grave 4,800 metres down, before doors in the ship's hull would swing open, swallowing it into hiding. But on the way up, disaster struck and a part of the claw snapped off. The crew managed to retrieve just half of the ship and no missiles were ever found.

Corporations are currently prospecting 1.3 million square kilometres of the seabed – about the size of Alaska. As the deep ocean belongs to nobody and everybody at the same time, the International Seabed Authority (ISA) was set up in 1994 to regulate seafloor activities in international waters. It currently has around thirty mining claims on its books in the Clarion-Clipperton Zone (CCZ) – a region of 75,000 square kilometres stretching across the Pacific from Hawaii to Mexico that is rich in nodules, seamounts and vents. At the moment, all activity in the CCZ is just in the experimental or exploratory phase, but that could soon change. A new rule book is currently being negotiated and should soon be released, signalling the start of seabed mining operations. But scientists are seriously concerned that mining could have disastrous consequences.

The problem is that we know very little about the ocean depths – it's often said that we know more about the moon. It's thought that many species in the deep ocean have yet to be discovered. Some might harbour valuable resources for new medicines. Others might be critical species in the deep-sea food web, supporting our fisheries and other species that mostly live in shallower waters. Indeed, one research team found evidence of grooves in the muddy seafloor 4 kilometres down, suggesting that whales might be diving to those depths in search of food.

Seamounts and polymetallic nodules can take many millions of years to form. If mining isn't carefully monitored, in just a few decades the creatures living on or around them could have their habitats wiped out. For example, nodules are the only hard surface for corals and sponges to grow on in the deep. Even if the situation is well managed, with just a certain quota of nodules, seamounts and vents allowed to be mined, creatures that have evolved in the quiet, dark waters of the deep would suddenly be exposed to light, and to noisy, vibrating equipment. Huge remotely operated mining machines would crawl across the seabed, kicking up clouds of dirt and smothering it in sediment. As the seabed helps to trap carbon and control ocean acidity, mining activity could also affect how the oceans aid in buffering climate change. So the race is on to investigate deep marine life before mining is given the go-ahead.

Once at the seabed, the ABYSSLINE respiration lander pushes three white plastic boxes into the sediment to measure how oxygen decreases over time, which indicates how active life is down there. Many of the organisms in the sediment are invisible to the naked eye, and yet, by monitoring how much oxygen and carbon they use, the scientists are gaining valuable insight into life at such depths, allowing them to compare their data with other areas of the ocean.

The expedition also hauled up from the deep all sorts of larger species, such as plankton and starfish. Although just over half of the creatures brought up were new to science, showing just how vital it is to log their existence before mining kicks in and species as yet undiscovered are lost to us for ever.

Maybe one day we'll recycle more of the metals in our gadgets, or there will be labels on the back of packaging to show where the materials came from. Yet, mining the depths may also be necessary to keep up with the growing demand by the renewables industry to make solar panels, wind turbines and electric car batteries. In the future, mining bodies in space, such as planets and asteroids, might save us having to resort to carving up the seabed. But, in the meantime, projects like ABYSSLINE are key to understanding the impact that mining would have on the mysterious and precious world of the deep ocean.

PROJECT MOHOLE

By the 1950s, the Space Race was hotting up. But while others were venturing way up high, a motley crew of scientists were hatching a plan to dig deep below the Earth's surface. Over a boozy breakfast, the so-called American Miscellaneous Society came up with the idea of drilling through the Earth's crust all the way to the layer of rock above the mantle – known as the Mohorovičić discontinuity.

Nicknamed the 'Moho', this layer was discovered by Croatian geologist Andrija Mohorovičić in 1909. His research showed that seismic waves, generated by earthquakes, travelled much faster below a depth of around 30 kilometres. This suggested that the rocks down there were different to the ones higher up.

Just as the *Apollo 11* crew brought back samples from the first moon landing, drilling to the Moho would provide geologists with pristine rock samples. We do already have rocks from the mantle, but these have been contaminated on their journey to the surface – a bit like meteorites that have passed through space on their way to Earth. There are rare so-called 'mantle nodules' which have erupted in volcanoes that show the mantle is rich in magnesium and poor in silicon minerals such as olivine and pyroxene. And there are pockets of former mantle rock that lie exposed on the seafloor, but they have been radically altered by seawater. The lack of fresh samples from the mantle mean that geologists struggle to be sure about even some basic facts, such as exactly what the mantle is made of, how it works and how it formed.

As the mantle lies at a depth of 30 to 60 kilometres on land, but only around 5 to 10 kilometres below the seafloor, the Project Mohole team found a suitable site at sea. But, before they started drilling, they had some significant challenges to overcome: they needed to secure funding and develop the technology to keep a drill ship stable over swelling waters – at that time there were no deep-sea oil rigs.

A system called 'dynamic positioning' was developed, whereby well-positioned propellers and thrusters kept the ship stable enough to drill down into the crust. This was no easy feat. Imagine lowering a piece of string the width of a human hair to the bottom of a 2-metre-deep swimming pool and then drilling 3 metres into the foundations.

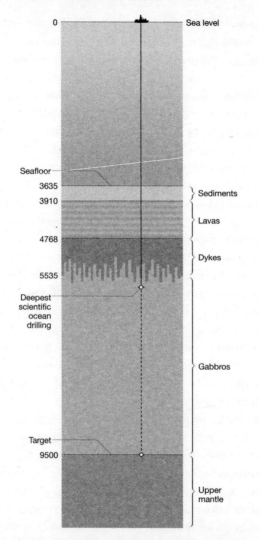

So far, the vessel *Chikyu* has drilled 3,262.5 metres below the seafloor. The aim is to reach the Moho

On the first drilling session, in 1961, off the coast of Guadalupe Island in the Pacific, the team succeeded in boring to a depth of 183 metres. But then disaster struck – funding was cut and the mission stalled.

Fast forward almost sixty years and a new team is attempting to drill to the Moho once more. The International Ocean Discovery Program (IODP) is made up of scientists from the UK, US, Germany and Japan.

Currently, the deepest depth the IODP team has drilled to is 3,262.5 metres below the seafloor – the world record for the deepest scientific ocean drilling. This is on board the vessel *Chikyu*, which is a specially designed drilling ship capable of boring to a depth of 7,500 metres below the seafloor in riser mode (10,000 metres in riserless mode). The riser is the bit of pipe that draws up sediment and rock.

Aside from netting some prize rock samples from the Moho, geologists hope that they will find evidence of subterranean microscopic life living at great depths. 'Extremophiles' living at those sorts of depths need to have a pretty impressive set of arsenal to cope with the extreme heat and pressure and virtually no nutrients. But single-celled microbes have been found in hydrothermal vents on the seafloor where temperatures reach a toasty 121 degrees Celsius. Another species can survive without oxygen. Another splits water from radioactivity in the rocks and so it feeds indirectly on radiation. Another grows in conditions more acidic than battery acid. And then there is the ultimate polyextremophile of them all. *Deinococcus radiodurans* can survive a multitude of extreme conditions – high doses of UV, desiccation, and ionizing radiation thousands of times greater than what would kill a human. No wonder it's been nicknamed Conan the Bacterium.

But, while lab microbes have been found to endure an amazing 1,000 atmospheres, temperature could be the killer. The upper limit for life is known to be 122 degrees Celsius, but geologists think Moho temperatures could be as low as 120 degrees. So, it's difficult to know what we will find deep beneath Earth's crust. While it won't be the giant prehistoric monsters dreamt up by Jules Verne in *Journey to the Centre of the Earth*, geologists could discover microbes that will help us to understand more about how life on Earth first began.

The man who spread the seafloor

From the deepest ocean trenches to the tallest mountains, the features on Earth's surface are partly moulded by forces deep within its belly. The tectonic plates that make up Earth's outer shell glide over the mantle, tearing apart or crashing together where they meet.

Back in 1912, Alfred Wegener proposed the idea of continental drift (see page 50), but no one knew what drove the process. It wasn't until the middle of the century that Princeton University geology professor Harry Hess came up with a viable theory. While sailing the high seas with the US Navy during the Second World War, Hess used the relatively new technology of sonar to map areas of the Pacific Ocean floor. What he found astounded him. Some of the deepest parts of the ocean were located near to continental margins, while shallower mid-ocean ridges were found in the middle of tectonic plates.

Hess came up with the idea that hot molten magma oozes out of mid-ocean ridges, expanding as it cools, pushing the seafloor apart in a process now known as seafloor spreading. To prove his theory correct, Hess and his colleague Walter Munk decided to try and retrieve some fresh mantle samples, and so they formed a team with the aim of drilling to the Moho – this became the ill-fated Project Mohole.

INTO THE TWILIGHT ZONE

The divers plunge beneath the surface, slowly sinking past shoals of brightly coloured fish and rocky outcrops with vibrant coral heads. The only sound in this tranquil tropical world is the occasional fish rippling through the water. As they descend further, the light starts to dwindle. The dive watch reads 20 metres – 25 metres – 30 metres. Below this depth lies the mesophotic zone – a gloomy, mysterious world stretching down to 150 metres, where just 0.1 per cent of sunlight filters down.

Until recently, very little was known about the mesophotic zone: scuba equipment wasn't advanced enough to work below 30 metres; and deep-diving tech, such as remotely operated vehicles and submersibles, was too large and costly to operate there. But, in recent years, this has changed with the advent of new technology enabling adventurous divers to explore below 100 metres. In closed-circuit rebreathers (CCRs) the air supply lasts longer than in regular diving equipment, as CCRs recycle carbon dioxide from a diver's exhaled breath, before mixing it with fresh pure oxygen. Plus, CCRs don't produce a noisy stream of bubbles, meaning divers disturb wildlife less.

This expedition in 2016 in the tropical waters of the Bahamas, led by scientists from the California Academy of Sciences, was one of the first times researchers have gone to such depths and was also key to understanding this relatively unknown part of the oceans, which is surprisingly rich in wildlife.

While the mesophotic zone covers only around 0.1 per cent of the oceans, it shelters almost one third of its biodiversity. Many of the species are unique to these depths, but some coral species that are common in shallow reefs are also found here, while some fish species swim between the two zones or are genetically similar to those at shallower depths.

Almost 75 per cent of the world's coral reefs are currently under threat from overfishing, habitat destruction, water pollution and climate change. Scientists know that global warming is seriously impacting shallow coral reefs around the world. More frequent storms result in more damage to fragile coral systems; changes in ocean currents interfere with their usual food supplies and dispersal of their offspring; more precipitation means that more freshwater runs off the land, flushing pollutants into the sea, which causes algal blooms that cut out vital light; rising sea levels causes more sediment to smother corals; more acidic oceans reduces coral growth rates and affects their structure; and warmer temperatures cause so-called 'bleaching'.

The polyps of most reef-building corals have what's known as a symbiotic relationship with photosynthetic algae called zooxanthellae that live in their tissues. The coral provide a safe haven and compounds needed for photosynthesis, and in return the algae supply them with the products of photosynthesis. But, in times of stress, the coral polyps can expel the algae, which means they lose their colour and turn white – becoming 'bleached' – and this can result in the coral dying.

The hope was that the mesophotic zone could be a saviour for some shallower reef species, helping to provide refuge when reefs become decimated closer to the surface. But recent research has questioned that theory.

At 30 metres down, the divers get to work – laying out quadrats and counting the species found within them. They swim on and repeat the process. Back on the surface, they discuss their first observations. Yes, there is some overlap between the deep and shallow reef fish species that they saw, but most of them prefer a specific depth. Top predators, such as sharks, which swim between the two zones, prefer to feed in the light, so are unlikely to take refuge in the deep.

Corals may fair better. Although they suffer from the same threats from human and natural impacts, such as an increase in storms, other research involving the relocation of coral fragments helped the species survive in the area.

Not only do corals like these provide a habitat for other species; they could also harbour previously unknown compounds that could be used as new antibiotics or other medicines beneficial to humans.

These research expeditions are some of the first to explore the previously unknown depths of the mesophotic zone. As almost all current reef management is biased towards shallow reefs, more expeditions like these could help to protect deeper reefs.

THE BIOPROSPECTORS

Taking the plunge into the bitterly cold Arctic water, the diver adjusts his mask before sinking beneath the waves. The drysuit keeps out the worst of the chill. The water gets murkier the deeper he goes. Scouring the seafloor, he spots a sponge and places it in a yellow mesh bag before collecting more samples to analyse later in the lab.

With water this chilly, there's got to be a really good reason to take the plunge. And there is. This is just one of many dives over the course of an expedition by a team from the University of Tromsø in Norway, who are part of a larger EU-funded project. The aptly named project PharmaSea is searching the largely untapped oceans for new drugs in the battle to beat the superbugs.

Bacteria are growing ever-more resistant to antibiotics. It's a vicious circle – the more we use antibiotics, the more bacteria develop resistance to them, the more people need them, the more we use them, the more bacteria develop resistance … At the moment, bacteria are gaining the upper hand. One researcher described it as becoming like the days before penicillin was discovered.

In the US, between 1997 and 2010, 60 per cent of sore throats were treated with antibiotics, despite the fact that only 10 per cent were caused by a bacterial infection. Action needs to be taken to limit the use of antibiotics. Yet we need to discover new ones. In Europe and the US alone, 50,000 people a year die from infections caused by resistant bacteria picked up during hospital stays. By 2050, 10 million people could die every year (roughly one every three seconds) because of antibiotic resistance. That is more than the death tolls of diabetes and cancer combined.

Easily accessible areas of the world on land and in shallow seas have already been scoured for species containing potentially useful medicinal compounds. That's why some researchers are turning their attention to polar regions and the deepest parts of the oceans.

Plant power

Some researchers have stayed on terra firma in their quest to find new cures. Ethnobotanist Dr Cassandra Quave is searching in rural Italy, quizzing locals about plants that have been used in traditional medicines for centuries. Some of the plant extracts she's identified work slightly differently to regular antibiotics that have been developed – they don't kill their targets, but instead inhibit microbial communication mechanisms. When bacteria reach a critical threshold, they communicate with one another via chemicals to start to attack the host. By stopping this 'conversation', bacteria can be made redundant. For example, Quave and her team have found that sweet chestnut leaf extract partly blocks the toxic effects of MRSA.

Inevitably, marine bioprospecting raises issues as to who owns what. The high seas start 200 nautical miles from land and are not owned by anyone. At the moment, the UN Convention on the Law of the Sea (UNCLOS) covers activities such as deep-sea mining and laying cables, but not bioprospecting. That is likely to change, as the situation is currently being reviewed. The big question is: should individual nations benefit from bioprospecting the high seas or should it be for the benefit of all humankind?

Back in the University of Tromsø lab, the samples collected by the divers are tested for various characteristics to find out whether they have antibacterial effects. If any do, the active compounds are isolated and their structures analysed with the hope of developing it into a potential new drug. Of course, this takes time – and yet time is running out. PharmaSea is just one of many projects around the world that are on the hunt for new compounds. Our lives are literally in the hands of these intrepid explorers who are raiding nature's medicine cabinet.

DRILLING INTO AN EARTHQUAKE ZONE

At 210 metres long and 130 metres high, the drilling vessel *Chikyu* is behemoth. On board there is space for 95 crew and 105 scientists, a helipad, a laboratory, living quarters, and the all-important drill and riser. (The riser is the bit of pipe that draws up sediment and rock.) The ship can drill to a depth of 7,500 metres below the seafloor in riser mode, and 10,000 metres in riserless mode – almost three times the height of Mount Fuji. The scientists on board are part of an international team investigating the cause of earthquakes.

The NanTroSEIZE International Ocean Discovery Program (IODP) has been running for over a decade, involving a number of ships at various different drilling sites. *Chikyu* has been anchored off the south-west coast of Japan, drilling into the Nankai Trough, where the Eurasian and Philippine Sea tectonic plates meet. It is one of the most seismically active spots on the planet and the source of many violent, large-scale earthquakes. While other projects around the world have drilled in areas prone to earthquakes, this one is aiming to be the first to dig down into the actual rocks where earthquakes develop in a subduction zone (see box).

As subduction zone faults are so vast, they generate huge earthquakes. In 1944, the subduction of the Philippine Sea plate caused the violent Tōnankai earthquake (which had an estimated magnitude of 8.1 on the Richter scale) that triggered a huge tsunami and devastated the Japanese coast. Earthquakes are commonplace in this part of the world, and the area is waiting for another big one to strike. So the need to understand more about quakes is urgent.

As the vast column of the riser is hauled up from the depths, some of the crew scurry around its base, pulling on various cables to manoeuvre it into the best position to then lay it flat along the deck. The riser has done its job and the scientists have a fresh batch of so-called 'cuttings' – the rock debris generated during drilling – to study in the on board lab. First up, the cuttings are washed and sieved to remove the drilling mud and separate out the rock fragments. They are then analysed in detail to find out useful information, such as what minerals they're made up of and how porous they are, in order to shed light on how the different rocks change with depth and the structure of the accretionary wedge (see opposite).

The IODP also aim to install sensors deep beneath the seafloor to record earthquakes as they happen, and hopefully reveal how water and rock interact at subduction zones. The more porous the rock, the more empty space there is between rock fragments

How an earthquake triggers a tsunami

At a subduction zone, two tectonic plates smash together. Where a continental plate collides with an oceanic plate, the latter gets forced down below the more buoyant continental one. Because of the friction between the two plates, the top layer of the subducting plate can get peeled back, forming what's known as an 'accretionary wedge'. The continental plate buckles under the pressure, rising up, then snapping as the tension becomes too much. As the continental plate rebounds, it generates an earthquake and a tsunami.

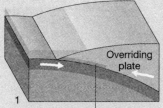

1
Friction locks the plates together

Overriding plate

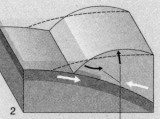

2
Slow distortion of overriding plate

Earthquake starts tsunami

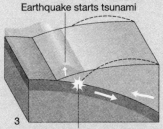

3
Locked area ruptures, releasing energy in the form of an earthquake

Tsunami waves spread

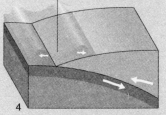

4

for water to fill. Usually, porosity decreases the deeper you go. But scientists think that more fluid than expected may exist at tectonic plate boundaries, reducing the friction between the plates and causing them to slip past one another. This will be the first time anyone has measured the fluid pressure at such depth.

The hope is that such data will provide new insights into the processes that cause earthquakes and will help to better forecast seismic hazards around the world before they cause mass devastation.

PART 4

SPACE MISSIONS

So much is known about our celestial neighbours that it's easy to forget just how far away they are – even on its closest approach, the moon is 363,104 kilometres from Earth. Since the launch of *Sputnik 1* in 1957, humans have sent thousands of spacecraft into the cosmos, revolutionizing our understanding of the solar system and beyond. Iconic missions such as the first moon landing have captured the news headlines, but other lesser known expeditions have also provided intriguing insights into our cosmic neighbourhood.

SPUTNIK 1

It has just passed midnight at the rocket launch site in Tyuratam, Kazakhstan. The date is 5 October 1957 and some of the Soviet Union's most celebrated rocket scientists are poised in a control bunker awaiting the launch of their latest project. With the push of a button the rocket's engines roar into life, blasting it into the night sky and taking with it a new kind of artificial satellite just months in the making. At exactly 314.5 seconds later, the satellite separates and a Soviet radio back on terra firma receives an affirming signal. *Sputnik 1* has become the first artificial satellite to reach Earth orbit. The Space Age has begun.

Much of *Sputnik 1*'s success can be traced back to the Cold War competition between East and West, which largely acted as a catalyst to technological advancements on both sides. Inspired by the V-2 rockets developed by German scientist Wernher von Braun during the Second World War, Soviet scientists had sprung into action at the war's end to develop their own intercontinental ballistic missiles (ICMBs) and keep the US within military reach. One of the key figures in Soviet rocketry was Sergei Korolev, who had designed the revolutionary R-7 ICMBs. The R-7 would eventually be developed into the Soyuz rockets that to this day continue to ferry US astronauts and Russian cosmonauts to the International Space Station.

Before *Sputnik 1* was conceived, the Soviets had attempted to develop a more ambitious satellite named Object D that would collect data on Earth's atmosphere, radiation from the sun and cosmic rays emanating from interstellar space. By the end of 1956, however, it became apparent that the project could not be achieved in time and, with knowledge of similar US ambitions, a simpler satellite was agreed upon. Mikhail Khomyakov, who was chief constructor at the Soviet's OKB-1 design bureau, was tasked with leading the design of *Sputnik 1*, and other key figures in the mission's development were Korolev and Mikhail Tikhonravov, the latter having been one of the earliest Soviet proponents of an artificial satellite launch. A bespoke version of the R-7 was developed, this time to carry not a nuclear warhead but instead a spherical science-gathering satellite.

For all its political and scientific significance, *Sputnik 1* was a rather modest design, at least in retrospect. Its shape was a result of two metal hemispheres joined with airtight sealing and fortified with thirty-six bolts. A 2-millimetre thickness was bolstered by a 1-millimetre-thick heat shield; and four radio antennas broadcast radio pulses back to Earth while an automated fan system prevented overheating. The science-gathering ambitions of Object D may not have been achieved, but *Sputnik 1* was able to collect data on the density of Earth's atmosphere – invaluable information to those in the business of engineering spacefaring rockets.

Sputnik 1's elliptical orbit flung it around Earth about once every ninety-six minutes, and Soviet scientists continued to track it for

Sputnik 1 in numbers

Launch date: 5 October 1957
Weight: 83.6 kilograms
Diameter: 58 centimetres
Orbital speed: 29,000 kilometres per hour
Number of Earth orbits: 1,400
Distance travelled: 70,000,000 kilometres

twenty-one days before its batteries died on 26 October 1957. On 4 January 1958, *Sputnik 1* fell back towards Earth, burning up as it passed through the atmosphere.

While Soviet reaction to the success of *Sputnik 1* was initially muted, the American response was predictably paranoid. The US had been busy building their own satellite, *Sputnik 1*, which would launch on 31 January 1958, but even before that a follow-up Soviet satellite named *Sputnik 2* had been successfully launched on 3 November 1957.

Meanwhile, on 6 December 1957, American citizens witnessed the failed launch of the Vanguard TV3, intended to be their country's first Earth-orbiting satellite. With the US feeling the might of Soviet success, in July of the following year President Eisenhower signed the National Aeronautics and Space Act, which would eventually bring NASA into being, and in September the National Defense Education Act was passed, providing low-interest loans for students studying maths and science. A new generation of young American scientists and engineers was born.

Sputnik 1 sent shockwaves around the world. Its relatively low orbit meant that even amateur astronomers with binoculars or a modest telescope could track it, while those with the requisite radio equipment could pick up its distinctive 'beep beep' signal as it passed overhead. At the UK's Jodrell Bank Observatory in Cheshire, radio astronomer Bernard Lovell was able to test out his new equipment by tracking the R-7 rocket that delivered *Sputnik* into orbit. Meanwhile, newspapers across the globe announced the dawn of a new spacefaring era.

For many, *Sputnik 1* was the catalyst that ignited the Space Race between the USSR and US. The Soviets' success demonstrated that it was possible to launch human-made satellites, and showed a rather complacent US just how far Soviet technology had come. The ramifications of *Sputnik 1* can be seen today in the Earth-orbiting International Space Station and Hubble Space Telescope, or the numerous spacecraft that explore the planets of our solar system and beyond. The Soviets had changed the course of world history, and had done so with a metal, beeping satellite about the size of an inflatable beach ball.

The Russian rocket man

Sergei Korolev is regarded as the father of Soviet rocketry and a key figure in the Soviet space race, even though he remained largely unknown during his lifetime. Born in 1907 in Ukraine, Korolev became engrossed in the fields of aerodynamics and rocketry and in 1931 co-founded the Group for Investigation of Reactive Motion, which worked on rocket development. The field was then still largely experimental, but Korolev would help bring it to the fore.

Despite his prowess, under the Stalinist purges Korolev was accused of treason and sabotage, and was sentenced to hard labour in 1938. But while in prison he continued his work on rocketry. In the 1950s, Korolev led the development of the R-7 rockets that evolved into the famous *Vostok*, *Voskhod* and *Soyuz* models, changing spaceflight for ever. His work helped the Soviets enjoy huge spacefaring success before he died of colon cancer in 1966. Just under three weeks later, the Soviet *Luna 9* became the first probe to soft-land on the moon, having been delivered by an R-7 derivative. While the USSR's failure to put humans on the moon before the US can't be wholly attributed to Korolev's absence, his death was clearly a major blow. Soviet secrecy meant that while Korolev's accomplishments were widely celebrated around the world, the man himself remained unknown until after his death.

THE FIRST HUMAN IN SPACE

'There in the flap you have dinner, supper and breakfast,' says Korolyov. 'You've got sausage, candy and jam to go with the tea. Sixty-three pieces – you'll get fat! When you get back today, eat everything right away.' 'The main thing is that there is sausage – to go with the moonshine,' jokes Gagarin. This is the last conversation between Russian chief rocket designer Sergei Korolyov and Yuri Gagarin, before the latter shouts '*Poyekhali*!' ('Let's go! We're off!'). The date is 12 April 1961. Strapped into a capsule on top of a *Vostok R*-7 rocket, Gagarin is about to make history and become the first human in space.

With the success of *Sputnik 1*, the Soviets had claimed the first victory of the Space Race, and for a few years at least they would remain ahead of the US in their endeavours. Nowhere was this more evident than the achievements of the young Soviet pilot, Gagarin.

But for all the fanfare and celebrity that would eventually come, Gagarin hailed from rather humble beginnings. Born on 9 March 1934 in a small village near Gazhtsk (later renamed 'Gagarin' in his honour), Yuri was the third of four children whose parents worked on a collective farm. In his early teens, a Russian Yak fighter plane was forced to make an emergency landing near Gagarin's home, leading him to take an interest in aeronautics and join a local flying club. He was later drafted into the Soviet Air Force, becoming a Senior Lieutenant by 1959.

The Soviet space programme had achieved a major coup with *Sputnik 1*, but the engineers of the USSR were already working on a new goal: putting a person in orbit around Earth and returning them safely. This branch of the space programme was known as Vostok, the same as the capsule and rocket, and would compete directly with NASA's Mercury programme.

The Soviet Union looked for cosmonaut candidates among its air-force fighter pilots because they would have the experience, strength and psychological stamina required of such an undertaking. Twenty candidates made it into the Vostok programme, eventually being whittled down to the 'Sochi Six'. By all accounts, Gagarin stood out among his peers and was credited with high intelligence and a strong character as well as a calm demeanour and warm smile. It also didn't hurt that he was relatively short at 157 centimetres (5 feet 2 inches), as the *Vostok* capsule was by no means spacious.

Gagarin's flight around the world lasted 108 minutes and saw him complete a single orbit, even bettering American astronaut Alan Shepherd's suborbital flight by about three weeks.

But recently declassified documents reveal the flight to have been anything but flawless. Just before take-off, engineers had to temporarily remove the spacecraft's hatch to mend a faulty sensor, while during the flight one of the R-7's engines failed to cut out at the intended time, taking Gagarin to life-endangering heights of 327 kilometres rather than the intended 230 kilometres. Transcripts show an increasingly frustrated Gagarin receiving evasive and vague answers from ground control as he inquired how the mission was going. Nevertheless, it was a success. Following his Earth orbit, Gagarin ejected from the spacecraft at 6,100 metres and parachuted back to Earth.

To say that Gagarin returned to Earth a hero would be an understatement. He was made a deputy of the Supreme Soviet of the Soviet Union, the highest legislative body in the USSR, and embarked on a world tour that included Germany, Brazil and Canada, among other countries. Gagarin had trained as a foundry worker, and accepted an invitation to visit from the Manchester-based Amalgamated Union of Foundry Workers in the UK. While being driven alongside a throng of cheering well-wishers through the streets of Manchester, Gagarin insisted that the hood of his car remain folded back and he stood up in the pouring rain as a mark of respect to those who had come to see him.

In 1967, cosmonaut Vladimir Komarov stepped up to command the flight of the *Soyuz 1* spacecraft, despite being aware of safety issues that would make it a potentially deadly mission. His fear was that Gagarin, his hero and mission backup, would fly instead and be killed in the process. Komarov lost his life when a parachute failed during re-entry, causing his spacecraft to crash to the ground, and he became the first person to die in the history of spaceflight. Paranoid Soviet officials reacted by banning Gagarin from future spaceflight missions, but this was in vain: the Soviet hero was killed during a routine training exercise when his fighter jet crashed on 27 March 1968.

The legacy of Gagarin and his groundbreaking mission lives on, and not just in the former Soviet Union. US *Apollo 11* astronauts Neil Armstrong and Buzz Aldrin left medals on the lunar surface commemorating Gagarin and Komarov, along with other astronauts who had lost their lives in the Space Race, and today 12 April is celebrated as both the International Day of Human Spaceflight and 'Yuri's Night'. But perhaps the most strange and touching tribute is one still undertaken by astronauts and cosmonauts alike as they make their way to the Baikonur Cosmodrome launch pad in Kazakhstan, where Gagarin's rocket launched all those years ago. Repeating Gagarin's own pre-flight actions, many a space-farer has been known to disembark temporarily from their vehicle and take a moment to urinate on the rear right tyre – possibly in the hope that Gagarin's good fortune might be with them as they strap themselves in for their own journey towards the stars.

THE FIRST SPACEWALK

In the cramped airlock of a Soviet spacecraft orbiting high above Earth, cosmonaut Alexei Leonov is waiting to make history. Beyond the thin shell of the craft, the cosmos awaits. He opens the hatch, makes his way outside and sees the bright, blue Earth rotating below him – continents and countries drifting past. The only thing protecting him from the vast universe is his spacesuit, which is tethered to a small spacecraft. Leonov has become the first human to spacewalk.

While the dangers of extra-vehicular activities remain, today they are part and parcel of space missions – indeed the International Space Station could not operate without them. But on 18 March 1965, Alexei Leonov achieved something no other human had done before. The *Voskhod 2* mission was another space race propaganda win for the Soviets, and another dent in US pride. And yet, Leonov and his pilot very nearly didn't make it.

Alexei Leonov was born in Siberia in 1934 and graduated as a fighter pilot in his early twenties, joining the class of cosmonauts that included Yuri Gagarin. In 1963, Soviet space architect Sergei Korolev announced that the next milestone was to have a cosmonaut float freely in space, and Leonov was the man to do it. Pavel Belyayev was selected as the pilot and the race was on, as the Soviets knew NASA was training astronaut Ed White for the same goal.

An R-7 rocket launched from Baikonur Cosmodrome to carry the cosmonauts into Earth orbit. Leonov put on his life-support system and climbed into the airlock, awaiting depressurization. He opened the hatch and clambered out to be greeted by the sight of planet Earth spinning in front of his very eyes. Leonov's movements were captured by a camera installed on the spacecraft, and after about ten minutes he was called back in. However, he was unaware of the journey that lay ahead.

Problems began when Leonov's spacesuit inflated due to a lack of atmospheric pressure, meaning he would not be able to fit back through the hatch. Unbeknown to mission control, Leonov opened a valve on his spacesuit to let air out. This was dangerous, but better than waiting for his oxygen to deplete. He was safe, at least for the time being.

The spacecraft was about to reach the unlit side of Earth, plunging it into darkness. Leonov pulled himself towards the spacecraft, but decompression sickness was starting to take hold, causing his temperature to soar. He flung himself through the hatch, although having entered head-first he would now have to manoeuvre in the cramped airlock to get the hatch closed. His helmet was drenched with sweat, but Leonov could just about see well enough to shut the door. He had made it, just.

The airlock would have to be jettisoned before the return journey, but the force of this procedure caused the spacecraft to spin. To make matters worse, oxygen levels rose dramatically, creating the potential for a single spark to turn their capsule into a fireball. Leonov and Belyayev got oxygen levels under control, but then realized their automatic re-entry system had failed. The cosmonauts would have to enter Earth's atmosphere manually, and any error could cause the spacecraft to plummet to the ground.

The talented duo completed the procedure, and their parachute brought them safely back down to Earth – but far from their planned landing site. Leonov and Belyayev surveyed their surroundings from the relative comfort of the module. Outside, a deep blanket of snow covered the ground. They had landed in the Siberian wilderness: a freezing, unforgiving world populated by wolves and bears.

They prised open the hatch of their module and the cold air rushed in. The pair sent out a signal for rescue and within hours a helicopter appeared overhead, but when they looked up they saw it was a civilian aircraft. Others had heard their signal and come to help. A dangling rope-ladder was not the rescue the cosmonauts had hoped for, as the heavy spacesuits would make climbing it impossible. More aircraft arrived: well-wishers dropping a bottle of cognac (that smashed), warm clothing (much of which became tangled in branches) and an axe.

Leonov and Belyayev realized they would have to spend the night in their spacecraft, but buckets of sweat in their spacesuits threatened frostbite. They stripped and poured the water from their suits, wringing their underwear dry before getting redressed. Next morning the rescue party arrived, but the cosmonauts would have to spend another night in the freezing forest. The rescue party constructed a wooden hut, chopped wood and a fire was lit to heat water and let the cosmonauts wash. The following day, the group donned skis and began the 9-kilometre trek to their rescue helicopter. Secrecy within the Soviet Union at the time meant the true story was initially not widely known. Nevertheless, it is an incredible tale of a milestone in human spaceflight – and subsequent human endurance.

There have now been over 200 spacewalks conducted from the ISS alone; and whatever spacewalks may achieve in future, their success will be owed to two cosmonauts who braved the threat of immolation, freezing temperatures and wild wolves, just to show the world that it could be done.

MAN ON THE MOON

The first warning sign blinks on the lunar module's computer just minutes into the landing sequence. Error 1202: data overload. As the two passengers look out the window of their spacecraft, the cratered surface appears tantalizingly close. More alarms follow before mission control affirms the 'OK' to land. The commander switches to manual control, but the module is over 335 metres beyond the intended landing site. Ahead lies a rugged, boulder-covered surface. The low-level fuel light flashes just as the commander spies a safe place to touch down, and he does so with forty-five seconds of fuel to spare. The time is 20:17:39 GMT on 20 July 1969. Humans have landed on the surface of the moon.

The chain of events that led to the *Apollo 11* moon landing arguably began with the USSR's *Sputnik 1* satellite, the first victory of the Space Race. Then, a year after Soviet Yuri Gagarin became the first man in space, in 1962 US President John F. Kennedy boldly stated that 'We choose to go the moon … and do the other things, not because they are easy, but because they are hard.' He was right, but the government's investment in a generation of young Americans would eventually pay off.

Apollo 11 commander Neil Armstrong's first spaceflight came in 1966 with *Gemini 8*, a precursor to the moon landing programme, while the mission's lunar module pilot was Edwin Eugene 'Buzz' Aldrin Jr, who had flown on *Gemini 12*, also in 1966. Previously Aldrin had been a fighter pilot in the Korean War, and was admitted into NASA's Astronaut Group 3 along with Michael Collins, who would become *Apollo 11*'s command module pilot.

The mission blasted off on a Saturn V rocket from Kennedy Space Center on 16 July 1969. Two hours and forty-four minutes later, a second burn sent *Apollo 11* on a course to the moon. The command and service module (CSM), which acted as living quarters for most of the mission, separated from the rocket stage containing the lunar module, known as 'Eagle'. Collins' job was to pilot the CSM and re-dock with Eagle before insertion into lunar orbit on 19 July. On 20 July, the CSM and Eagle separated, the former continuing to orbit the moon and the latter, with Armstrong and Aldrin inside, beginning the descent to the lunar surface. Collins was now a lone astronaut aboard a small vessel on the far side of the moon, cut off from humanity, gazing out into the vast abyss beyond.

On 21 July at 02:56:15 GMT, Armstrong's foot made contact with the lunar surface, and a live transmission broadcast the event to an estimated 530 million people globally. He uttered the famous words, 'That's one small step for man, one giant leap for mankind.' Twenty minutes later, Aldrin followed. One of the first tasks was to collect a small lunar sample for return, in case an emergency would cut the mission short. In total, the astronauts spent two hours, thirty-one minutes and forty seconds walking on the surface of the moon, traversed about one kilometre and collected 21.5 kilos of samples, straying only as far as 60 metres from the lunar module. A camera recorded their activities, and Armstrong and Aldrin would also take a call from US President Nixon during the mission. They erected a US flag and planted a plaque that read: 'Here men from the planet Earth first set foot upon the moon July 1969, AD. We came in peace for all mankind.'

Sheets of aluminium foil were deployed to collect data on the solar wind – a stream of plasma and charged particles that emanates from the sun. Scientists could study the embedded chemical composition more clearly given the moon's lack of substantial atmosphere, and the results would indicate the effect of Earth's magnetic field on the solar wind, revealing new insights about our home planet.

At 17:54:00 GMT on 21 July, the lunar module lifted off and re-docked with *Columbia*. The service module was jettisoned and the spacecraft re-entered Earth's atmosphere at 36,194.4 feet per second, a parachute slowing its descent into the Pacific Ocean at 16:50:35 GMT on 24 July. Quarantine completed, the astronauts received a hero's welcome as they paraded through New York City, but they would never fly into space again.

The making of a moonwalker

Flying was one of Neil Armstrong's greatest passions. Born in 1930 in Ohio, he took his first flight with his father aged six years old, then received his pilot's licence at sixteen and became a naval air cadet by 1947. After studying aeronautical engineering and serving in the Korean War, in 1955 Armstrong became a research pilot for the National Advisory Committee for Aeronautics (later NASA), flying advanced aircraft like the X-15, a rocket-powered plane that could reach speeds of over 6,400 kilometres per hour.

He became an astronaut and entered the space programme in 1962. On 16 March 1966 Armstrong commanded the *Gemini 8* mission, the first-ever manual docking between two spacecraft. During the mission the spacecraft went into a fast spin, and Armstrong had to steer a controlled splashdown into the Pacific Ocean.

After *Apollo 11*, Armstrong resigned from NASA in 1971 and taught aerospace engineering until 1979. While many Apollo astronauts went into politics or joined the autograph circuit, Armstrong instead elected to inspire a new generation of pilots. He was also appointed to the body that looked into the Space Shuttle *Challenger* accident in 1986 (see page 187).

There is a sense among many that NASA's human space programme never returned to the glory days of Apollo, when a generation of young Americans dared to imagine the impossible. Today, there is talk of returning to the moon; even of building a permanent settlement from which to launch new missions (see page 251). But whatever the future may hold, humanity will forever look back to that summer, decades ago, when a group of young Americans were just about arrogant enough to think they could conquer another celestial body, and just about crazy enough to pull it off.

VOYAGER 2

Humanity's only mission to the outer planets of the solar system might never have occurred had it not been for a young NASA intern stumbling upon a rare planetary alignment. Gary Flandro was at NASA's Jet Propulsion Laboratory in 1965 when he realized that by the late 1970s Jupiter, Saturn, Uranus and Neptune would all be on the same side of the sun, and would not be so again for another 176 years.

In 1961, another NASA intern named Michael Minovitch had undertaken groundbreaking research into the 'gravity assist' method of using a planet's gravitational pull and orbital movement to propel spacecraft, and Flandro was able to build on this work to propose a mission to the outer planets. With gravity assists, the time to reach Jupiter and Saturn could be halved, while the journey to Uranus and Neptune could be reduced to a third. All four could be visited in a single mission. NASA was convinced, and *Voyager* was born.

Originally, two pairs of spacecraft were to be used, but budget restrictions meant that NASA eventually settled for a single pair to explore Jupiter and Saturn. *Voyager 2* launched on 20 August 1977 and was followed on 5 September by *Voyager 1*. The latter would overtake its twin and explore Jupiter and Saturn, while *Voyager 2* would provide follow-up observations. *Voyager 1* would duck out of the solar system after Saturn, but a proposed mission extension would allow *Voyager 2* to also visit Uranus and Neptune. The *Pioneer 10* and *11* missions in the early 1970s had made initial steps in investigating Jupiter and Saturn, but the Voyagers would provide more detailed views of these planets (plus Uranus and Neptune) – and reveal incredible phenomena never seen before.

Voyager 2 is the only spacecraft to have studied all four outer planets at close range. It flew by Jupiter on 9 July 1979 and revealed atmospheric changes that had occurred since *Voyager 1*'s encounter. The latter had revealed Jupiter's moon Io to be volcanic, and *Voyager 2* was able to gather more information about the active volcanoes. *Voyager 2* also managed to get more detailed images of Jupiter's moon Europa, resolving streaks seen by *Voyager 1* into cracks that would later be interpreted as evidence of a subsurface ocean below its icy crust (see page 242).

A gravitational boost at Jupiter fired *Voyager 2* to Saturn, which it flew closest to on 26 August 1981 and observed the star Delta Scorpii through the planet's rings. The flickering starlight enabled *Voyager 2* to discover tiny ringlets, and the spacecraft also captured images of moons Hyperion, Enceladus, Tethys and Phoebe.

After NASA decided to extend its mission, *Voyager 2* flew by Uranus on 24 January 1986, where it found evidence of a boiling ocean 800 kilometres below the cloud tops, measured the atmospheric temperature at a chilly −216 degrees Celsius, and discovered ten new moons and two rings. But maybe most exciting of all, it observed the planet's aurorae – magical light displays just like the Southern and Northern Lights seen around the poles on Earth.

The next target was Neptune, which it flew by on 25 August 1989, discovering five moons, four rings and a huge, dark storm in the planet's atmosphere. The spacecraft measured winds of 1,100 kilometres per hour and revealed Neptune's largest moon, Triton, to be the coldest known planetary body in the solar system, with frozen volcanoes erupting nitrogen ice.

Its final encounter complete, on 5 November 2018, *Voyager 2* bid au revoir to the solar system, just like its twin had done before it on 25 August 2012. Both spacecraft are now zipping through interstellar space sending back data – and expected to do so until about 2025. But each is equipped with a 'Golden Record' containing music, sounds and greetings from Earth. They include images of our planet and its inhabitants hidden within audio signals, as well as instructions on how to play the records and the cosmic location of our solar system. So, even after the Voyagers run out of fuel, the spacecraft and their Golden Records will stay on course; cosmic relics from a lone inhabited planet, journeying out towards the stars.

The Voyager missions were deemed a huge success. *Voyager 1* gave its science team many firsts and provided an unprecedented look at Jupiter and Saturn, their moons, atmospheres, rings and magnetic fields, picking out areas of interest for *Voyager 2* to follow up. It also became the first human-made object to reach interstellar space, making its mission a milestone in spaceflight history. But the missions are probably most celebrated for their close-up images of the planets and other bodies in the solar system. Although perhaps the most well-known image produced is the exact opposite – one in which our own planet appears as an almost indecipherable dot against the backdrop of space.

The idea for *Voyager 1*'s solar system family portrait was a collaboration between US astronomer Carl Sagan and Carolyn

Porco, who would later command the *Cassini* mission's imaging team (see page 225). NASA chiefs initially scoffed at the idea of wasting precious resources on a scientifically useless image of Earth and its planetary neighbours, but Sagan and Porco pushed for it until permission was granted.

The result was not much to write home about from an imaging perspective but Sagan, ever the humanist, turned it into a treatise on the fragility and isolation of planet Earth and its inhabitants. Pointing to the image of Earth, which he dubbed the 'Pale Blue Dot', in 1994 Sagan made a speech at Cornell University in which he asked us to consider: 'That's here. That's home. That's us. On it,

Space volcanoes

For Linda Morabito, the morning of 9 March 1979 began just like any other on Voyager's navigation team. She was sitting alone in the image processing room at NASA's Jet Propulsion Laboratory, analysing a *Voyager 1* image of Jupiter's moon Io, when she noticed a bright object on the moon's limb. Although she didn't know it for certain, Morabito had discovered an active volcano. For those precious moments, she had seen something on another celestial body that no other human had seen, and it was a matter of time before her discovery was confirmed.

We now know that Io is the most volcanically active world in the solar system, where some of the many volcanoes shoot lava up to 400 kilometres into the atmosphere. But other active volcanoes have been spotted elsewhere in the solar system, such as on Saturn's moon Titan, where so-called 'cryovolcanoes' fire out cold liquid or frozen gases such as water, ammonia or methane, instead of lava.

everyone you ever heard of, every human being who ever lived, lived out their lives … on a mote of dust, suspended in a sunbeam.'

The mission had given planetary scientists the initial reconnaissance of our planetary neighbourhood, but for Sagan it was a chance to remind us all of the futility of our existence, in the hope that we might instead learn something about ourselves.

THE SPACE SHUTTLE

It's early morning on 12 April 1981 and a new kind of spacecraft, decades in the making, is sitting on the launch pad at Kennedy Space Center. Rocket boosters thrust the spacecraft into the air, its nose pointed towards the sky. About eight minutes later, the spacecraft has reached Earth orbit. It is twenty years to the day since Yuri Gagarin became the first man in space, and NASA has just launched humanity's first reusable rocket: the Space Shuttle.

On board are *Apollo 16* moonwalker John Young and navy test pilot Robert Crippen. Up until this moment, everyone who has ever flown into space has done so on a single-use rocket that would crash and burn and a space capsule that would return to Earth charred and scorched. Young and Crippen, on the other hand, intend to land their Shuttle, and NASA intends to relaunch it.

Orbiting Earth at speeds of about 28,000 kilometres per hour, computers on board the first flight of Shuttle *Columbia* record temperatures and pressures during launch, orbit and re-entry. The astronauts test the payload bay doors to demonstrate the Shuttle's ability to transport and collect cargo. About fifty-five hours and thirty-six orbits later, Young pilots the orbiter to touch down at

Edwards Air Force base in California. Mission STS-1 is complete, and the era of the Space Shuttle has begun.

The Shuttle was intended to usher in a new era of space travel. In total, five shuttle craft were used over the years: *Columbia*, *Challenger*, *Discovery*, *Atlantis* and *Endeavour*. *Columbia* was the first to launch, on 12 April 1981, and *Atlantis* was the last to land, on 21 July 2011. In total, 355 individuals flew on 135 missions over a period of thirty years.

The Shuttle launched the Chandra X-ray and Hubble Space Telescopes and the Compton Gamma Ray Observatory, also allowing astronauts to revisit Hubble and continually upgrade its hardware over the decades. It launched the Galileo probe to study Jupiter, the *Magellan* spacecraft at Venus and the *Ulysses*

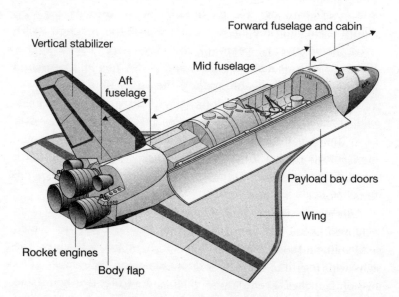

Forward fuselage and cabin

Vertical stabilizer

Mid fuselage

Aft fuselage

Payload bay doors

Wing

Rocket engines

Body flap

mission to survey the sun. It helped construct and service the International Space Station.

The Shuttle era saw Sally Ride become the first American woman in space and Kathryn Sullivan the first American woman to spacewalk, while Mae Carol Jemison rode the Shuttle to become the first African-American woman to reach Earth orbit.

Young and Crippen's inaugural flight certainly launched three decades of firsts for NASA; but, even on this important mission, anomalies would foreshadow tragedies yet to come. Inspections showed damage to the external heat shield tiles designed to deflect temperatures as high as 1,600 degrees Celsius generated during re-entry. Sixteen tiles were lost and 148 were damaged during this first mission, and similar issues remained throughout the programme.

On 28 January 1986, *Challenger* broke apart in the air 73 seconds after launch, killing its crew. An O-ring seal in the right booster had failed, allowing leakage of burning gas. On 16 January 2003, a piece of foam insulation broke off *Columbia*'s external tank during launch and struck its left wing, cracking its heat shield. On 1 February 2003 during re-entry, hot atmospheric gases penetrated *Columbia*'s cracked shield, causing the spacecraft to break apart. Its crew of seven were killed. Both disasters led to pauses in the programme and, after the launch of *Discovery* on 26 July 2005 – the first since the *Columbia* disaster – the programme would last just six more years before it was discontinued.

Criticisms of the programme are not uncommon. The cost per weight to launch was actually higher than those of expendable spacecraft, and some argue that NASA repeatedly ignored warning signs with regard to the Shuttle's safety, instead favouring timely mission launches. Even despite this, the Shuttle flew on average about five times a year: hardly the reliable, regular spacecraft that had been billed. But regardless of how the Shuttle is remembered, the programme was an epoch in human spaceflight, the reverberations of which – good and bad – will be felt for decades to come.

Shuttle success stories

The *Challenger* and *Columbia* disasters should not supersede the Shuttle programme's many successes. *Discovery*, *Atlantis* and *Endeavour* each played a huge role in the development of spaceflight.

During its thirty-nine missions, *Discovery* carried Eileen Collins the first female Shuttle pilot, John Glenn the oldest astronaut and Bernard Anthony Harris Jr the first African-American spacewalker. It became the first spacecraft to retrieve a satellite and bring it back to Earth, and in February 1994 Russia's Sergei Krikalev become the first cosmonaut to fly on the Shuttle.

Atlantis carried out twenty-three missions, during which it launched the ATLAS-1 microgravity science laboratory – the first phase of a NASA project to study the science of our own planet from space – and achieved the inaugural Shuttle dock with the Russian Mir space station. In May 2009, *Atlantis* ferried astronauts for the last-ever mission to service the Hubble Space Telescope.

Endeavour was the last Shuttle to launch, having been constructed as a replacement following the *Challenger* disaster. During its inaugural flight the first ever three-person spacewalk took place. In December 1998, it left a lasting imprint on modern spaceflight, delivering the first US module during the construction of the International Space Station.

THE HUBBLE SPACE TELESCOPE

On 24 April 1990, the Hubble Space Telescope was launched into Earth orbit by Space Shuttle *Discovery*, and was deployed a day later. Yet when its first images finally appeared, they were blurry due to a fault in the primary mirror. How to repair a 13-metre-long telescope orbiting 27,350 kilometres per hour, 550 kilometres above Earth? This was the task that faced NASA optical engineer James Crocker as he visited Munich to liaise with the European Space Agency. Crocker looked up at the shower head in his hotel bathroom, noticing how it could be slid up and down and tilted as needed. Crocker's epiphany that day saved the mission and with it decades of groundbreaking astronomy yet to come.

One of the major problems with terrestrial astronomy is Earth's atmosphere. This barrier protects life on Earth, absorbing the sun's UV rays and minimizing temperature extremes between day and night. But the atmosphere is a nuisance for ground-based telescopes because it distorts light from distant stars and galaxies. In 1946, US astrophysicist Lyman Spitzer Jr extolled the benefits of a telescope that would operate beyond the atmosphere and, in 1977, US Congress approved funding for what would become the Hubble Space Telescope. In 1993, the first Space Shuttle mission to service Hubble implemented Crocker's solution, and astronomers could get on with observing the cosmos.

Hubble has changed much of what we know about the universe, from helping to determine its age to providing views of star formation within beautiful spiral galaxies and evidence of black holes. One of its first successes was an observation of Supernova 1987A, an exploded star in a satellite galaxy of the Milky Way known as the Large Magellanic Cloud. Astronomers were able to measure the diameter of a ring of material around the supernova and refine the distance to the LMC within a 5 per cent accuracy: 169,000 light years.

In 1994, Hubble made the first confirmed detection of a supermassive black hole at the centre of a galaxy during observations of M87, 50 million light years away. In April 2019, astronomers released an image of the same supermassive black hole, captured by the Event Horizon Telescope: the first time a black hole had ever been photographed. Astronomers now theorize that nearly all massive galaxies have central supermassive black holes.

In 1995, the iconic 'Pillars of Creation' image showed newborn stars radiating within the glowing cosmic clouds of the Eagle Nebula. In 1996, the Hubble Deep Field image revealed 1,500 galaxies within a small portion of the sky. This feat was bettered in 2004 with the Hubble Ultra Deep Field, which revealed over 10,000 galaxies, some nearly as old as the universe itself.

In 1998, Hubble astronomers published their observations of Type Ia supernovae. These exploding stars shine with the same luminosity, so their apparent brightness is used to calculate distances in the universe. The study provided further evidence that the expansion of the universe is accelerating, rather than slowing down.

The telescope has even peered back in time by observing so deep it can see light from the birth of the universe. In 2016, Hubble scientists were able to observe an infant galaxy as it existed 13.4 billion years ago, 400 million years after the Big Bang.

Hubble has also observed objects closer to home. In the early 1990s, it captured images of Jupiter's Great Red Spot and observed fragments of comet Shoemaker-Levy 9 impacting into the gas giant. It produced the first-ever images of surface features on Saturn's moon Titan and detected oxygen on Jupiter's moon Europa, as well as potential water vapour plumes on Europa in 2012, which suggested a subsurface ocean ripe for investigation. It discovered moons around

The man who changed the universe

In 1919, the American astronomer Edwin Hubble took up a post at the famous Mount Wilson Observatory in California, where he would make one of the greatest discoveries in the history of science. The accepted wisdom was that our galaxy was the only galaxy in the universe; those other, fuzzy deep-sky objects were gassy regions known as nebulae. However, in 1923 Hubble discovered what's known as a Cepheid variable star in the Andromeda Nebula. Comparing the star's known brightness with its observed brightness, Hubble concluded it was 1 million light years away; beyond the calculated boundary of our galaxy. The Andromeda Nebula was in fact the Andromeda Galaxy; another like our own, meaning that there must be more galaxies beyond the Milky Way. Not only that, but Hubble's subsequent galactic observations revealed that the universe is expanding. Around four decades after his death in 1953, a new generation of US astronomers searched to name their new space telescope. In deference to the astronomer who had turned our view of the universe on its head, the Hubble Space Telescope was born.

Pluto, rings around Uranus and in the early 2000s provided the first visual evidence of planetary building blocks in orbit around a young star.

In 2001, Hubble was used to make the first direct measurement of the atmosphere of an exoplanet: a planet orbiting a distant star. In 2007, it detected hazes in another exoplanet's atmosphere, showing that it could be used to search for biomarkers that might indicate signs of life on the surface. Between 2016 and 2018, it observed the atmospheres of the newly discovered seven rocky Earth-sized exoplanets orbiting star TRAPPIST-1 and was able to track asteroid Oumumua, the first known interstellar object to pass through our solar system.

Aside from its wealth of scientific discoveries, Hubble's influence on humanity has been immense. Its name has entered common parlance and its images have found their way into popular culture. For how much longer the mission will last is currently unknown but, when it finally ends, Hubble's legacy will be over 1 million observations and over 15,000 peer-reviewed science papers, as well as reams of data ripe for making future discoveries. The universe is a vast unknown, and the Hubble Space Telescope has made it feel a little smaller and a little less mysterious, but more thrilling than we could ever have imagined.

THE HUNT FOR A NEW HOME

Perched in a natural crater and surrounded by lush rainforest, the radio telescope on a remote mountainside in Puerto Rico looks like the entrance to a Bond villain lair. But, in 1992, the 300-metre-wide dish helped Polish astronomer Aleksander Wolszczan make an incredible discovery.

At the time, it was malfunctioning and out of action for most research. This was fortunate for Wolszczan as it meant he had free reign to continue with his search for pulsars – stars that emit regular radio pulses. When checking out one particular star, something appeared to be wrong. He thought the equipment must be playing up. After a while he started to realize that something was blocking the view. Intrigued, he eventually worked out what was causing the interference: two planets were orbiting the star. Never before had anyone 'seen' an extra solar planet – also known as an exoplanet. This groundbreaking glimpse opened the floodgates for the discovery of thousands more exoplanets over the years.

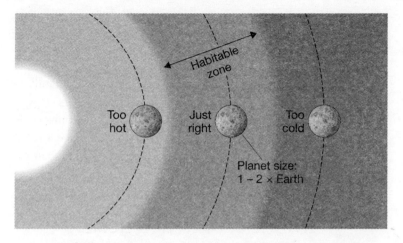

Too hot

Just right

Too cold

Habitable zone

Planet size: 1 – 2 × Earth

The habitable zone around a star where conditions are ideal for life

Launched in 2009, the Kepler Space Telescope monitored 145,000 stars until 2013 when it packed up. But in that time it helped identify hundreds of exoplanets – and a few that scientists think could be similar to Earth.

The 'Goldilocks zone' or 'habitable zone' is the area around a star where conditions are just right to support liquid water on orbiting planets. Liquid water equals the possibility of life. If a planet orbits too close to a star, water will boil away. Too far and it will freeze. So the key is to find a planet where water pools on its surface – a rocky planet like Earth.

Now, a new raft of spacecraft is picking up where Kepler left off. The James Webb Space Telescope (JWST) will launch in 2021 (see page 244). But NASA's Transiting Exoplanet Survey Satellite (TESS) and the European Space Agency's CHEOPS (CHaracterizing ExOPlanet Satellite) are already in action.

Exoplanet ID

Size

When a planet passes in front of its host star, it dims the star's light. Using space-based telescopes, such as CHEOPS, astronomers can use this transit method to work out a planet's size.

Composition

When a planet passes in front of its host star, some starlight passes through its atmosphere. By analysing the different colours in the light using the transit method, it's possible to work out what a planet is made of. Carbon dioxide or methane would suggest the existence of life.

Mass

An Earth-based telescope can calculate the mass of a planet by seeing how much the star 'wobbles', indicating the planet's gravitational pull. The more massive a planet, the greater its mass and the stronger the gravitational force that it exerts on other bodies near it.

TESS is using its four wide-angle telescopes to scan the skies, surveying half a million stars in the hope of finding exoplanet candidates similar to Earth. Meanwhile, CHEOPS is looking in detail at exoplanets that have already been identified – either Earth-sized planets or ones whose size is roughly somewhere between a gas giant like Jupiter or Saturn and a rocky planet like Earth or Neptune. These so-called super-Earths or super-Neptunes will give us an idea of whether water, and hence life, could exist on a rocky world larger than our own.

An exact Earth twin hasn't yet been spotted. But a number of potential cousins have been identified – the most Earth-like are Kepler-186f and Kepler-62f. Kepler-186f is around 1.1 times the size of Earth, while Kepler-62f is more of a super Earth at 1.4 times. Only time will tell whether these missions can find a planet like our own – another habitable world to call home.

LANDING ON A COMET

It is 20 January 2014 and, not far from the orbit of Jupiter, a small spacecraft awakes from a three-and-half-year hibernation. Its twelve-year journey across the solar system is nearly complete: soon it will arrive at an ancient 4-kilometre-wide comet. Rosetta will become the first probe to orbit a comet's nucleus, and in doing so may just reveal how the solar system came to be.

Comets are icy, rocky relics left over from the formation of the solar system 4.6 billion years ago and, as such, are one of the best chances of studying the physical and chemical processes that occurred during that period. How did the planets form? What role did comets play in the development of life on Earth? Did they transport water to our planet? Answers to many fundamental questions may lie in the data collected by the European Space Agency's Rosetta spacecraft.

In August 2014, Rosetta hitched a ride with its comet companion, known as 67P/Churyumov-Gerasimenko, in the cold, outer reaches of the solar system and followed the comet as it neared the sun on part of its six-and-a-half-year elliptical orbit.

In November 2014, the spacecraft released its small Philae lander, which descended to the surface of the comet to make a soft landing. But it didn't quite go as planned. Harpoons and ice screws failed, and the lander bounced off the surface before landing in a different, much darker region. Miraculously, the lander was relatively unharmed, and still managed to collect data.

A close-up image of the Philae lander on the comet's surface

A month before the mission's end, Rosetta finally located Philae wedged into a dark crack. Lack of sunlight meant that the lander was under pressure to gather data before its solar-powered batteries ran out; but the fact that it landed on more than one location was actually something of a bonus, allowing comparison between the sites. Philae analysed the chemical composition of the comet's gas and dust, including samples thrown up during its first touchdown, revealing sixteen different organic compounds. It detected water vapour, carbon monoxide and carbon dioxide in the gases of the comet's coma (which gives it its fuzzy appearance), as well as chemical compounds that are known to play a key role in the formation of ingredients essential for life.

As Philae's future lay in doubt, Rosetta meanwhile remained in orbit at 67P and began to study it, imaging its surface topography to reveal huge cliffs and boulders. The most striking thing about 67P is its 'rubber duck' shape, which Rosetta discovered was a result of two smaller comets having collided in the early solar system.

The spacecraft found organic chemicals on 67P, including the amino acid glycine, related to proteins, and phosphorous, a component of DNA and cell membranes. In other words, the ingredients for life. It also found molecular oxygen, nitrogen and water, although not like water found on Earth, or even on other comets.

The elliptical orbit of 67P brings it close to the sun and, as it does so, heat causes its water ice to sublimate into water vapour, which jets particles of dust into space. Rosetta was able to analyse these gas and dust particles, and revealed that comets can be geologically active bodies with energetic, internal processes generating surface eruptions.

Following 67P on its approach to the sun gave scientists a unique look at how the comet's seasons change over time. For most of its orbit, 67P's northern hemisphere has a five-and-a-half-year summer, but months before it reaches perihelion (its closest point to the sun) – it's the southern hemisphere's turn for a brief summer. These seasonal changes cause small dust particles to be transferred across the comet, creating dust showers. Rosetta was able to collect and study these particles, which may be related to the interplanetary dust that coalesced into larger particles in the early solar system, as comets began forming.

Rosetta recorded growing fractures and surface changes like weathering and erosion, as well as stresses in the comet's structure caused by both the release of gas and the comet's spin. All of these sculpt the landscape and cause it to change over time. Rosetta was also able to give scientists an idea of what comets smell like. The combination of ammonia, hydrogen cyanide and hydrogen sulphide makes for an interesting olfactory cocktail: not unlike urine.

In September 2014, scientists spotted a 70-metre-long fracture on a 134-metre-high cliff named Aswan. As the comet got closer to the sun, sublimation increased, dragging more dust out into space.

Rock 'n' roll Rosetta

Despite the major scientific successes of missions like Rosetta, it's safe to say they are not widely known to the public and do not generally receive the mainstream media coverage you might expect considering their revelations about to the origins of the solar system. One of the key figures in bringing Rosetta's accomplishments to the fore has been Dr Matt Taylor, the mission's London-born project scientist. Taylor's colourful Hawaiian shirts, tattoos, lively sense of humour and penchant for death metal make him a well-known personality among space and science fans, and just the kind of person to show that astrophysics can still be 'cool'. Yet the attention paid in some quarters to Taylor's personality and fashion sense often drowns out his contribution to this important mission.

As Rosetta project scientist, his job was to liaise with and support the various teams to ensure that the science objectives of the mission were met, and that the most was made of the reams of data collected by the two spacecraft. Taylor has also been key to communicating Rosetta's successes to the wider public. Anyone attending one of his entertaining presentations can expect to learn a lot about cometary science, participate in a group selfie on Twitter, and leave having sampled the back catalogue of metal bands like Cannibal Corpse and Napalm Death.

An outburst was seen on 10 July 2015 and, days later, a sharp edge was seen on the cliff where the fracture had been, while boulders were spotted at the cliff's base. Had Rosetta just witnessed a gaseous outburst on a comet causing one of its cliffs to collapse? The mission showed that, rather than being static objects of dust and ice, comets are geologically interesting worlds.

In September 2016, beaten, bruised and nearly out of fuel, Rosetta made a controlled descent to join Philae on the surface of the comet, and eventually its transmission to Earth fell silent. No one quite knows what happened to it. Perhaps the spacecraft has been lost to space, or perhaps it still remains on the comet, weathering the seasonal changes and dust showers of an ancient piece of the solar system as it journeys around the sun.

NEW HORIZONS

NASA New Horizons scientists received their first truly tantalizing glimpse of Pluto on 8 July 2015: a blurry image revealing a heart-shaped feature, captured by the *New Horizons* spacecraft from a distance of 8 million kilometres. On 14 July it would fly 12,500 kilometres above Pluto's surface and over the coming months, glorious views of the feature – a glacier 1,000 kilometres wide – would emerge, beamed to our planet by a spacecraft operating 5 billion kilometres from the sun.

When the spacecraft launched on 19 January 2006, its destination was the outermost planet in the solar system. By the time it got there, Pluto had been reclassified as a dwarf planet – a planetary-mass object orbiting the sun, but that doesn't quite meet the criteria to be defined as a true planet.

Nevertheless, the mission revealed the secrets of this outer world and its moons like never before. It showed Pluto to be geologically complex, boasting mountain ranges, deep pits and icy structures.

The ages of different surfaces on the dwarf planet vary dramatically. Craters point to regions 4 billion years old – almost as old as the planets themselves – while others such as Sputnik Planitia are smoother and therefore younger, perhaps 10 million years old. This region forms the western lobe of Pluto's heart-shaped glacier, and *New Horizons* found it to be a deep basin containing frozen nitrogen, methane and carbon monoxide. Perhaps this basin formed via a large impact, or maybe ice built up over time and sank deep into the terrain. Either way, its young age suggests geological activity on Pluto.

New Horizons spotted cellular ice features, some measuring 50 kilometres across, that may be younger than 1 million years old. These cells are smoother in the middle and rougher around the edges: evidence of heat causing the convective flow of nitrogen ice to rise at the centre and descend at the rim. Dunes of methane ice particles the size of grains of sand were found in the mountains surrounding Sputnik Planitia, probably formed by wind and aided by the sublimation of ice into vapour, which dislodges the grains.

Frozen methane might sound odd, but not on Pluto. *New Horizons* discovered huge blades of methane ice stretching hundreds of feet tall. Scientists think methane freezes on to the terrain, then sublimates in some areas to leave behind colossal structures. *New Horizons* also found methane ice-capped mountains in Cthulhu Macula, south-west of the heart-shaped region. Between the mountains are deep valleys a few kilometres across and tens of kilometres long. The surface is a rusty red colour, indicating organic materials called tholins produced when sunlight reacts with the frozen methane.

The same process may explain a dark red polar cap on Pluto's largest moon, Charon. *New Horizons* also found a huge, deep canyon system on the moon's eastern limb, bigger than the Grand Canyon at 700 kilometres long and 9 kilometres deep. Observations of Pluto's smaller moons Nix, Hydra, Styx and Kerberos suggest water ice on every one, implying that the moons were all formed from the same collision billions of years ago.

Water ice was also discovered on Pluto; specifically on its highest-known mountain range Tenzing Montes, in Sputnik Planitia. The highest peak is about 6 kilometres tall, and scientists infer they must be made of water ice rather than methane, as only water could form such tall structures without collapsing. Other tall features known as Wright Mons and Piccard Mons appear to have holes on their summits, suggesting they could be ice-erupting cryovolcanoes; another possible sign of geological activity.

New Horizons also discovered a beautiful blue atmosphere on Pluto, whose haze was seen to vary in illumination by about 30 per cent. This change in brightness could be caused by air flow over Pluto's mountain ranges.

The mission at Pluto complete, *New Horizons* was assigned a new task; a flyby of the Kuiper Belt Object called Ultima Thule. So, on 31 December 2018, while others were gearing up for New Year revelries, NASA scientists were prepping for *New Horizons'* encounter with the celestial object. On 1 January 2019, the spacecraft raced past it at 51,000 kilometres per hour. It was the most distant flyby ever achieved.

Kuiper Belt Objects are a ring of rocky bodies beyond the orbit of Neptune, left over from the formation of the solar system, and studying them is vital to our understanding of the origins of the planets.

Pluto's planetary debacle

In 2006, the International Astronomical Union addressed the wealth of newly discovered bodies in our solar system by redefining the term 'planet'. As a result, Pluto was reclassified as a dwarf planet, leaving our solar system with just eight planets and sparking a debate that continues to this day. Among those who disagree is Alan Stern, principal investigator of the *New Horizons* mission.

Stern asks us to look at Pluto. It has an atmosphere, mountain ranges, tectonics, glaciers, avalanches. Are these not planetary traits? What of the worry that there might be too many planets for school children to memorise? This is unscientific, Stern argues. There are more than eight rivers, mountains or chemical elements in the world.

The IAU says a planet must clear its orbital path – in other words, it has to be the dominant gravitational body in its orbit around the sun – but further from the sun it's more difficult for a body to do so. Were Jupiter more distant, Stern says, it would cease to be a planet.

He points to asteroids that fly close to Earth. Can we say Earth really clears its orbital path? If not, can our own planet still be described as such? The debate is unlikely to end any time soon, but while the IAU definition stands, both Pluto and those in favour of its planetary status will continue to find in Alan Stern an influential and eloquent advocate fighting their corner.

At Ultima Thule, *New Horizons* discovered a 35-kilometre-long snowman-shaped object of two flat lobes that probably merged in the early solar system. It is likely the objects once orbited one another and gravity pulled them closer over time. The flyby revealed interesting pits – one of which is 8 kilometres wide – that could be a result of impacts, or ice sublimating out into space, lost due to Ultima Thule's low gravity and lack of atmosphere. There is evidence for methanol, water ice and organic molecules on the surface. So the hope is that Ultima Thule and its Kuiper Belt companions might hold the key to how life emerged on Earth. By 2020, all the data should be fully available and scientists can complete the story of this primordial cosmic body.

The *New Horizons* spacecraft is now continuing on its journey out into the cosmos. It will eventually fall silent and join the *Voyager* and *Pioneer* spacecraft as another scientific relic from Earth drifting through interplanetary space.

THE DAWN MISSION

Between the orbits of Mars and Jupiter, some 400,000,000 kilometres from the sun, lies the asteroid belt; a dusty ring of rocky relics left over from the formation of the solar system. Some asteroids are the size of boulders, others may be a few kilometres wide, but the largest is a dwarf planet known as Ceres, just under 1,000 kilometres in diameter. Around this rocky body is a lonely, now-defunct spacecraft that is destined to orbit it for decades to come.

The spacecraft was launched from Earth in September 2007 to study the two largest of these cosmic building blocks and in doing so reveal clues about planetary formation and evolution – even how the solar system itself came to be. The spacecraft would help piece together the story of our cosmic origins and was named, appropriately, *Dawn*.

Ceres and Vesta are the largest and second-largest objects in the asteroid belt respectively, and make up about 45 per cent of its total mass. But they are fundamentally different. Vesta is rocky like the inner solar system planets Earth and Mars, whereas Ceres is distinctively icy, more like the outer solar system moons. When *Dawn* arrived at Vesta in 2011 it became the first spacecraft to orbit a body in the region between Mars and Jupiter. In 2015, when it arrived at Ceres, it became the first human-made spacecraft to visit a dwarf planet.

All the other dwarf planets we know of exist beyond the orbit of Neptune on the edge of the solar system, so Ceres offered a unique opportunity to study a specimen much closer to Earth. In total, *Dawn* made 3,000 orbits around Ceres and Vesta, and revealed a wealth of fascinating information.

The mission showed that dwarf planets may once have hosted oceans in their ancient past, and could potentially have them even today. It mapped Ceres and Vesta's cratered terrain, building complete pictures of their composition, temperature, mass, gravity and rotational axis, as well as the chemicals present on their surface.

Orbiting Vesta between July 2011 and September 2012, the spacecraft beamed back images of craters, canyons and mountains. It studied a 500-kilometre-wide crater known as the Rheasilva Crater, thought to have formed from an impact with another asteroid about 1 billion years ago. This collision may have scattered debris from Vesta, and this debris eventually landed on our planet in the form of meteorites. The spacecraft confirmed a category of meteorites that make up 5 per cent of all meteorites found on Earth, known as howardites, eucrites and diogenites (or HEDs), originate from Vesta.

Dawn also revealed that Vesta's northern hemisphere is peppered with large impacts – more than expected – suggesting there were more large objects in the early asteroid belt than once thought. It discovered mysterious dark spots that may be the result of impacts by carbon-rich material from elsewhere in the solar system. Vesta was found to be a layered, rocky world with steep slopes and landslides exposing fresh material; a fascinating geology on an ancient asteroid.

After Vesta, *Dawn* moved on to Ceres, arriving in 2015. While there it discovered over 300 spots of bright material on its surface, most of which are associated with impact craters like the 92-kilometre-wide Occator Crater. These spots point to the presence of salty ice below the dwarf planet's surface, and suggest that Ceres may once have had a global ocean. The bright material was likely deposited via sublimation of water ice directly into water vapour, and it is possible that there may still be briny liquid rising to the surface today.

Bright streaks were also spotted on Ahuna Mons, a now-inactive cryovolcano on Ceres's equator that would have spewed up salty water and mud in its past, instead of lava like volcanoes on Earth. The fact that Ahuna Mons has a sharp peak suggests it is relatively young – potentially just a few hundred million years old – as it has not been eroded over time. *Dawn* also revealed Ceres has a layered internal density, which could point to dense rock having settled below the dwarf planet's water-rich crust during its evolution.

Possibly most exciting of all, though, was that the mission detected organic materials around the northern Ernutet Crater that, coupled with the evidence of Ceres's wet past, means it may once have had conditions to support life, and may still do today. The discovery of ammonia suggests that materials on the dwarf planet – or perhaps even the dwarf planet itself – originated in the outer solar system. Was Ceres an outer body that was pushed into the asteroid belt? If so, does this explain why it is so similar to the outer icy moons?

On 31 October 2018, *Dawn*'s transmissions fell silent and the following day NASA scientists announced that the spacecraft had run out of fuel. The mission was over. Given the potential for life-supporting conditions on Ceres, *Dawn* was left in orbit for at least twenty years, before it will eventually crash on to the dwarf planet: long enough that any bacteria from Earth still on the spacecraft would be wiped out by the extremities of space. NASA couldn't risk contaminating Ceres: it is too precious. It's just possible that the body may contain vital clues as to how life in our solar system began.

MAPPING DEEP SPACE

**'Dix, neuf, huit, sept, six, cinq, quatre, trois, deux, un ...'
Lift off. A huge inferno belches from beneath the rocket as it starts its ascent, roaring up through the sky, eventually disappearing from view behind the clouds. On board is an instrument that will radically enhance our knowledge of the universe and what happened after the Big Bang.**

Around 13.8 billion years ago, the universe existed as an opaque fog of particle-filled plasma that was so dense not even light could penetrate it. It continued to expand and cool until, about 380,000 years later, the first atoms formed and the universe became transparent. A few hundred million years later still, the first stars formed. Leftover radiation from this period continued spreading across the universe, and is now known as the cosmic microwave background (CMB).

This phenomena was unintentionally discovered in 1964 by American radio astronomers Robert Wilson and Arno Penzias when their equipment picked up an unexplained static noise. The pair tried relentlessly to explain it, including removing pigeon droppings from their antennae, but to no avail. Eventually they turned to the scientists at nearby Princeton University, who revealed its source to be the CMB, and in 1978 Wilson and Penzias won the Nobel Prize in Physics for their discovery. Today, astronomers know that the CMB fills all of space, and observing its distribution is one way of building a picture of the universe as it existed just after the Big Bang.

A key mission in understanding the CMB was the European Space Agency's Planck observatory (named after German physicist Max Planck). The highly sensitive space telescope was launched on 14 May 2009 and orbited Earth from a distance of 1.5 million kilometres. It was deactivated on 23 October 2013.

The CMB cannot be seen by human eyes, so it's up to telescopes like Planck to do the observing for us. One of Planck's major goals was to measure fluctuations within the CMB and discover how these correspond to the variations in density that eventually grew into the massive galaxies and galaxy clusters that we see today. It was also tasked with investigating the nature of dark matter. This mysterious substance cannot be directly observed, but its existence is inferred by its gravitational effect on visible matter like stars and galaxies which, incidentally, account for just 5 per cent of the total matter in the universe.

Current models suggest that just seconds after the Big Bang, the universe went through a period of rapid expansion known as 'inflation', and one of Planck's science objectives was to study how this was triggered, but also whether the process generated warps in space-time called gravitational waves.

Planck was by no means the first mission to study the CMB, as NASA's COBE (1989–1993) and WMAP (2001–2010) probes had already done so, but it promised greater accuracy than ever before, measuring signals 10 per cent fainter than WMAP had achieved.

Planck operated not unlike an ordinary telescope. Its 1.9- by 1.5-metre primary mirror collected faint light from the CMB, while a large 'baffle' both cooled the telescope and prohibited unwanted stray light. Its two main instruments, the High Frequency Instrument and the Low Frequency Instrument, converted the light into maps of the microwave sky. Planck was able to detect variations in CMB temperature a million times smaller than one degree, revealing the 'seeds' that eventually grew into galaxies and clusters.

So what did Planck actually discover? One of its biggest achievements was the creation of the first all-sky map of the CMB. It also revealed that dark matter makes up about 26.8 per cent of the known universe; a higher value than had previously been calculated.

The data changed the timescale of the so-called 'epoch of reionization': that moment when the first light spread across the cosmos. Initial estimates in 2003 suggested this occurred about 200 million years after the Big Bang, but Planck's data moved this date much later, suggesting that the universe was already halfway through reionization when it was 700 million years old. It provided evidence for inflation in the early expansion of the universe, and showed that our current model of the universe is largely on the right track. But it also showed that anomalies remain.

One of the crucial discoveries has been of asymmetry in the average temperatures of the CMB across the sky. You might expect that the universe would be largely the same all over, but this is not the case. An asymmetrical 'cold spot' in temperature had already been detected by the WMAP mission, but Planck's more sensitive instruments cemented the anomaly, which has not yet been explained.

Further, Planck's measurement of the Hubble Constant – the rate of expansion of the universe – doesn't quite agree with measurements by the Hubble Space Telescope and ESA's Gaia mission: another discrepancy that has yet to be solved.

In science-gathering missions, research will always continue long after the conclusion of the mission itself, and we can expect more discoveries to be made over the coming years: Planck's final data set was released on 18 July 2018 and threw open many of these unresolved anomalies. Perhaps most significantly, it showed that astronomers have come a long way in our understanding of how the universe formed and evolved, but that there is clearly a lot more work yet to do.

EXPLORING MARS

Ripping through space at 5,800 metres per second, the capsule holding the Curiosity rover enters the thin Martian atmosphere. Mission control back on Earth hold their breath. This is the most complicated rover landing ever attempted.

Around 10 kilometres above the rocky red surface the parachute deploys, slowing the capsule to 470 metres per second. The heat shield pops off, then the parachute and back shell detach. Immediately the pyrotechnic devices fire up, slowing the descent to 100 metres per second. The rover dangles precariously below the so-called 'sky crane', edging closer to the surface. Then, just 392 seconds after entering the Martian atmosphere, the rover touches down.

Rocky, arid and bitterly cold, Mars is a hostile place even for machines. Temperatures range between 30 and −140 degrees Celsius. Huge dust storms can circulate around the whole globe. And yet, since landing in 2012, Curiosity has been exploring Mars' inhospitable surface, sending a stream of data and incredible images back to Earth.

The size of a car and able to travel at up to 90 miles per hour, it weighs 899 kilos and is kitted out with numerous cameras and different bits of specialized equipment to analyse the surface of the Red Planet. Powered by plutonium, it communicates with Earth via a series of small satellites that orbit Mars.

Curiosity has been key in some big scientific discoveries – such as soil analysis showing clear evidence for water on Mars, and the likelihood that the planet once had more oxygen in its atmosphere.

The rover has outlived its two-year life expectancy and continues to roam the planet. But it's not alone in its quest to uncover more of Mars' secrets. In the skies, orbiters such as the *Mars Odyssey* and *Express* analyse the planet's geology, climate and mineralogy.

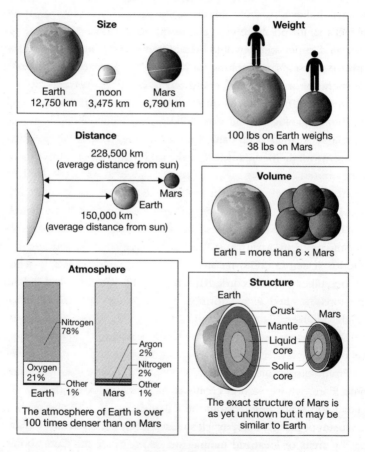

Mars vs Earth

The big hope is that one day we will find evidence that life once existed on Mars. On Earth, all forms of life need water, so the search is on for areas where liquid water was once stable, as well as looking below the surface, where it might exist today. Indeed, a radar instrument on board the Express orbiter has spotted what is believed to be a lake trapped beneath the surface on the planet's south polar ice cap. Life also needs energy to survive. As so-called 'superoxides' would break down organic molecules on the surface, missions are looking for life deep underground – powered by chemical or geothermal energy, as opposed to sunlight.

In 2021, a new rover is due to land on Mars that will search for the building blocks of life by drilling down into its surface. This ExoMars rover has been named Rosalind Franklin, after the scientist whose work helped James Watson and Francis Crick reveal the structure of DNA.

In the meantime, the newest addition to the fleet – *InSight* – is investigating the deep interior of Mars. On board *InSight* are numerous probes used to measure its 'vital stats', such as its 'pulse' (seismology). In April 2019, the lander's Seismic Experiment for Interior Structure (SEIS) recorded its first likely 'marsquake'. While 'moonquakes' were recorded by instruments left from the Apollo missions, the Red Planet formed in a different way to our lunar neighbour. Hence, these marsquakes should reveal more about how the solar system's rocky inner planets formed, as well as shedding light on why Mars doesn't have a magnetic field.

From seismic data on Earth we know our planet has a liquid outer core, whose motion creates a magnetic field, enveloping the planet and protecting us from the lethal radiation of the solar wind (a stream of plasma and particles from the sun). Mars seems to have patchy areas of localized magnetism. *InSight*'s seismic data should reveal whether the Red Planet has any liquid core remaining, which is vital to understanding how to protect future Martian colonists from deadly radiation.

Manned missions to Mars are on the horizon (see page 211). Maybe one day intrepid astronaut explorers will find evidence of life on the Red Planet. In the meantime, rovers and orbiters give us an incredible insight into this intriguing neighbour.

A YEAR IN SPACE

High above rural Kazakhstan, a spacecraft is falling through the sky. On board are US astronaut Scott Kelly and cosmonauts Mikhail Kornienko and Sergey Volkov. Their *Soyuz* capsule undocked from the International Space Station three hours ago and is now racing through Earth's atmosphere. About fifteen minutes before landing, parachutes deploy and help the *Soyuz* make a cushioned touchdown on terra firma. For Kelly and Kornienko, it is a particularly momentous occasion. They have just spent 340 days straight on the International Space Station. The date is 2 March 2016.

The International Space Station is in constant freefall. However, its trajectory means it always dips over Earth's horizon, putting it in a circular orbit around the planet. As a result, astronauts on board the ISS are also in a state of constant freefall, creating a state of weightlessness for the duration of their mission. The space industry still has much to learn about how spaceflight affects the human body – not just in terms of weightlessness but also the isolation and claustrophobia that come with it, not to mention increased exposure to radiation. What is the physical and psychological impact of spaceflight? What about the circulatory and digestive systems, or reason and decision making? Many detrimental effects are already known, such as muscle and bone degradation, while some astronauts return to Earth with worsened eyesight. Most ISS missions are six months, but getting to Mars alone could take even longer than that. How can we prepare astronauts for mammoth journeys across the solar system? Kelly and Kornienko's One-Year Mission was designed to help answer some of these questions. It was by no means the longest-ever stay in space, but Kelly's position in particular was unique. He and his brother Mark are the only identical twin astronauts in history, offering the opportunity for a groundbreaking experiment. Both Scott and Mark underwent tests before, during and after the mission, with Mark remaining on Earth and acting as a control.

The results of the One-Year Mission are not yet fully realized, but some discoveries have already been made. In Scott, scientists noted a change in gene expression, which is how genes react to changes in the environment. After six months back on Earth, 7 per cent of these changes had not returned to normal in Scott, suggesting spaceflight may have consequences for the body's immune system, DNA repair and bone formation. Scott also lost weight, fluids swelled in his head and scientists noted a change in the shape of his eyeballs.

Studies were also made into the telomeres in Scott's body. These are the ends of chromosomes and they shorten as the body ages. But in Scott's case they became longer and then a majority re-shortened within two days of his return to Earth. Scientists observed no real decrease in his cognitive performance during tests before and after the mission, but they did note a decrease in mental speed and accuracy.

The tricky part is working out how much of this is due to the environment of space, and how much is down to a change in lifestyle. Astronauts on the ISS have restricted calorie intake and a rigorous exercise regime, while post-landing fatigue and re-adapting to Earth's gravity may also have played a part.

The study didn't take up all of the mission time, however. Astronauts on the ISS carry out numerous scientific experiments that contribute both to our understanding of spaceflight and the workings of the universe. Kelly and Kornienko saw the arrival of a new instrument, the CALorimetric Electron Telescope (CALET), whose purpose is to study the mysterious substance known as dark matter. They helped deploy mini satellites and Kelly drew blood, provided urine samples, looked after growing crops, logged his activities and sleep patterns and completed three spacewalks to carry out physical upgrades to the space station.

Ultimately, Kelly and Kornienko's mission confirmed that the human body can reasonably withstand a year in space, opening up the door for even longer missions. With commercial space companies and NASA now aiming to send humans to Mars, it is important to find out whether the astronauts would be able to survive such an epic journey. Either way, the One-Year Mission is a stepping stone towards that end – taking those first steps on the surface of the Red Planet.

Who has spent the most time in space?

Scott Kelly may hold the record for consecutive days in space by a US astronaut, but Russian Valery Polyakov holds the world record, having spent 438 straight days on the Mir space station between 1994 and 1995. NASA astronaut Peggy Whitson spent 289 days on the ISS between 2016 and 2017 and has notched up a total of 665 days in space throughout her career, giving her the women's record for consecutive days and the US record for accumulated days. The US men's record for total time in space is 534 days, held by astronaut Jeffrey Williams. Russian cosmonaut Gennady Padalka holds the world record, with a whopping 879 days spent in space over five different missions. Kelly and Kornienko's accumulated time totals are 520 and 516 days respectively.

ASTEROID SAMPLE MISSION

The idea of autonomous robots hopping about on an asteroid 300 million kilometres from Earth might seem like the work of science fiction, but not if you've been paying attention to one of the Japan Aerospace Exploration Agency's (JAXA) current missions.

Hayabusa2 was launched by JAXA in December 2014 to collect a sample of an asteroid and return it to Earth for analysis in late 2020. On 26 February 2018, *Hayabusa2* took its first image of its target, a near-Earth asteroid named Ryugu, and on 27 June 2018 it arrived at its 'home position', 20 kilometres from the rocky body. The US also has an asteroid sample-return mission currently in operation named OSIRIS-REx, which is set to return a sample of the asteroid Bennu in 2023 (see box on page 219).

Asteroids are like time capsules from the early solar system, and studying them can teach scientists about the origins of the planets that orbit the sun. Small pieces of asteroids fall to Earth as meteorites, but are contaminated by the time they reach the ground. Ryugu is thought to contain organic matter and water and has probably not changed much since the formation of the solar system, 4.6 billion years ago. What better way to study a cosmic relic in its purity than by landing robots on it, or returning uncontaminated samples to Earth? *Hayabusa2* intends to do both.

The mission is a follow-up to JAXA's first Hayabusa mission, which returned samples of asteroid Itokawa to Earth on 13 June 2010. However, that mission's MINERVA lander failed to land on its target, instead tumbling out to space when it was launched from the spacecraft.

Hayabusa2 is the first mission to land a rover on an asteroid. Its MINERVA-II1 lander deployed on 21 September 2018 and consisted of two rovers, each 18 centimetres wide by 7 centimetres tall and weighing 1.1 kilos, dropped by the spacecraft from a height of 60 metres. Because Ryugu's gravity is so weak, wheeled rovers would be ineffectual and so these rovers hop about the surface, flying through the air for fifteen minutes at a time and moving as far as 15 metres with each hop. They can autonomously decide what data to gather and beam back up to *Hayabusa2*, which then transmits it to Earth. They have cameras to build a picture of the asteroid's surface, plus temperature and optical sensors.

On 2 October 2018, *Hayabusa2* deployed its MASCOT lander on to Ryugu. This cube-shaped 10-kilo hopping rover can take images and measure temperature, but is also equipped with a spectrometer to analyse the composition of the asteroid and instruments for measuring magnetism and radiation.

Hayabusa2 wasn't about to let its landers have all the fun. On 21 February 2019, the spacecraft touched down on Ryugu. During its brief contact it fired a 5-gram bullet of the element tantalum into the asteroid, scooping up ricocheted fragments into its sample catcher. The bullet was made of tantalum so that scientists can distinguish it from asteroid samples when they come to study *Hayabusa2*'s bounty back on Earth. During the first Hayabusa mission, a similar bullet failed, but the spacecraft was still able to return a few asteroid particles. *Hayabusa2* is aiming for 10 grams of material, although this will not be confirmed until scientists open up the catcher and look inside.

In April 2019, *Hayabusa2* deployed its Small Carry-in Impactor: a probe loaded with explosives that was sent to the surface of Ryugu to generate a large crater, exposing fresh material uncontaminated by the solar wind and the radiation of the solar system. *Hayabusa2* made a 'safe retreat' to avoid being caught in the blast, later returning to inspect the crater and confirm the operation a success. Not only will this provide fresh material for analysis, but also enable scientists to learn more about the composition of the asteroid, and how it reacts to being struck by an impactor.

What JAXA scientists see when they open up *Hayabusa2*'s sample collection in 2020 is anyone's guess, but they should find scientifically valuable, potentially organic material from the early solar system. Analysis could reveal clues as to the formation of our planet, where our water came from, or even how life arose on Earth. Whatever the outcome, future generations will look back with reverence on a plucky Japanese spacecraft that journeyed out into the solar system and brought a piece of it back.

OSIRIS-REx

The US OSIRIS-REx mission launched on 8 September 2016 and rendezvoused with asteroid Bennu on 3 December 2018. Since then it has been mapping the asteroid's surface to find a suitable site from which to collect a sample in 2020. The sampling arm will make contact with the asteroid's surface for about five seconds, releasing a burst of nitrogen gas that will stir up surface material into the sample head. It has the ability to undertake three sample attempts, and could collect as much as two kilos worth of material. The mission objectives are much the same as *Hayabusa2*'s, but it is likely that asteroid Bennu will impact Earth in the late twenty-second century, so studying it may help scientists devise potential deflection methods for pushing space rocks out of harm's way. OSIRIS REx is due to land back on Earth on 24 September 2023, and 75 per cent of its sample will be preserved for research worldwide, including by future generations of scientists.

JUNO: MISSION JUPITER

The date is 4 July 2016. Across the United States, families and friends celebrate the anniversary of their country's independence. But in a windowless room in Pasadena, California, a group of planetary scientists sit poised with bated breath. At 8.53 p.m. local time, the room erupts into a loud cheer as colleagues jump from their seats, embrace one another and shout with joy. The building is NASA's Jet Propulsion Laboratory, and *Juno* mission scientists have just witnessed their spacecraft complete its five-year journey and enter orbit around the planet Jupiter.

Jupiter is a fascinating world. The gas giant is the biggest planet in our solar system and twice as massive as all the other planets combined. Its atmosphere is made mostly of hydrogen and helium and it is covered in storms, the largest of which is a gigantic cyclone about twice the size of Earth known as the Great Red Spot. Its stripy appearance is a result of light-coloured zones and darker belts, caused by differences in the chemical composition and movement of gas in the atmosphere.

Before *Juno*, the only other dedicated mission to study Jupiter was *Galileo*, which orbited the gas giant from 1995 until 2003. *Juno* was designed to probe deeper than ever before and reveal insights into the planet's formation and evolution. The spacecraft launched from Earth on 5 August 2011 and since arriving at Jupiter has performed elliptical orbits of the planet, flying above the cloud tops and probing below the surface to reveal clues about its core, atmosphere, aurora displays, magnetic and gravitational fields.

To discover the secrets of Jupiter, *Juno* is equipped with a fleet of science instruments including cameras to capture images of the planet in optical, ultraviolet and infrared light. *Juno* spins three times per minute, enabling it to stabilize but also allowing each of its instruments a sweep of Jupiter's surface, while solar panels provide power even though the mission is taking place so far from the sun.

The spacecraft's fifty-three-day elliptical orbit takes it over Jupiter's north and south poles and includes one close pass during which it flies as close as 5,000 kilometres above the cloud tops, taking just two hours to get from pole to pole. Despite this, it still manages to avoid Jupiter's most intense radiation zones. Initially, *Juno* was supposed to perform a manoeuvre in October 2016 that would bring it on to a path of closer fourteen-day orbits until the mission's conclusion in February 2018, but issues with helium check valves meant the manoeuvre was too risky, and NASA decided to retain the fifty-three-day orbit. It would take longer to gather the data but the larger orbit would lessen the spacecraft's exposure to radiation, meaning the mission could be extended until July 2021.

So far, *Juno* has not disappointed. It has provided incredible images of the planet's stormy atmosphere, homing in on swirling clouds and murky blue polar regions that look nothing like the Jupiter we are familiar with. The mission has revealed the gas giant to be a tempestuous planet with Earth-sized polar cyclones that reach speeds of 350 kilometres per hour and are like nothing else seen in the solar system. It also found that the belts and zones that give Jupiter its stripy appearance penetrate 3,000 kilometres below the surface, yet beneath the stormy atmosphere the planet probably rotates as an almost rigid body. In July 2017, the spacecraft flew 9,000 kilometres above the Great Red Spot, providing a closer view of it than ever before and revealing that the storm penetrates 300 kilometres into the atmosphere.

Juno has also revealed that Jupiter has a strong non-symmetric magnetic field, 20,000 times stronger than Earth's, that shows variations between the planet's northern and southern hemispheres. It has recorded energies of up to 400,000 volts at the planet's poles producing the most powerful auroral displays in the solar system: ten to thirty times the energy that produces Earth's aurorae (the magical light displays of the Southern or Northern Lights seen around the poles). Observations of Jupiter's poles also revealed that most of the planet's lightning storms occur there, rather than at the equator like on Earth, showing the benefits gained by *Juno*'s polar-centric orbit. Many of these discoveries have yet to be fully explained, suggesting that Jupiter has further secrets lying in wait.

On 21 December 2018, *Juno* made its sixteenth flyby of Jupiter, completing its global coverage of the planet and marking the halfway point of the mission. But the spacecraft has a lot of work yet to do. Further data should reveal more information on the generation of Jupiter's magnetic field, what lies beneath its surface, and how the planet has evolved over time.

The *Juno* mission has so far shown Jupiter to be a fascinating and complex planet, perhaps more intriguing than planetary scientists had expected. While the spacecraft has already made many discoveries, its data will be studied long after the mission's conclusion in 2021. Until then, scientists will eagerly follow the remainder of its time at Jupiter, which will end when *Juno* performs a controlled de-orbit into the planet's atmosphere and bids the gas giant and its satellites a fond farewell.

EXPLORING THE RINGED PLANET

It is 22 April 2017, and a lone spacecraft is orbiting Saturn's largest moon, Titan, just over a billion kilometres from Earth. But the moon is not the object of its study; at least not today. The aim is to use Titan's gravitational pull to alter the spacecraft's trajectory, firing it through a 2,000-kilometre gap between the cloud tops of Saturn and its iconic rings. It grazes the rings as it speeds through the gap at 120,000 kilometres per hour. The spacecraft is named *Cassini*, and it has just completed one of the most daring manoeuvres of the Space Age.

NASA's Cassini-Huygens mission launched on 15 October 1997 and entered orbit at Saturn on 1 July 2004. The mission consisted of an orbiter named *Cassini* that studied the planet and its moons, and a lander named Huygens that detached on 25 December 2004 and parachuted safely on to the surface of Titan.

Titan is one of the most Earth-like places in the solar system, boasting an atmosphere and rain showers of liquid methane that form rivers and lakes, just as water does on our own planet. When the Huygens probe landed on Titan it became the first human-made spacecraft to safely touchdown on a body in the outer solar system. During its 2.5-hour descent and 72-minute transmission on Titan's surface, Huygens beamed back data on its atmospheric density and pressure, measuring temperature variations between −100 and −203 degrees Celsius. Huygens also detected winds of 430 kilometre per hour and confirmed that the atmosphere consists primarily of nitrogen and methane. It found evidence of geological activity and 100-metre-deep ravines with steep valley slopes on Titan's rugged terrain.

Meanwhile, on the main mission, *Cassini* was the first spacecraft to ever orbit the ringed planet. It completed 294 orbits of Saturn and

162 flybys of its moons, travelled 7.9 billion kilometres and captured 453,048 images. It sent back data on the planet's weather, gave us close-up glimpses of its moons – as well as discovering seven more – and studied Saturn's iconic rings.

It revealed that the icy, rocky rings are probably relatively new, between 10 and 100 million years old, compared to Saturn itself, which is about 4.5 billion years old. *Cassini* measured the rings' gravitational tug, which enabled *Cassini* scientists to calculate their low mass. Coupled with the rings' brightness, the results revealed the structures are relatively uncontaminated by cosmic debris, leading scientists to infer their age.

Cassini also discovered and imaged features in the rings appropriately named 'propellers', due to their shape. These features, some of which are thousands of kilometres long, are created by tiny moonlets orbiting within the ring system itself, pushing away material as they do so. Some moons, like Pan, actually create a gap in the rings as they orbit. Pan was imaged orbiting in a 325-kilometre-wide channel in Saturn's A-ring known as the 'Encke gap'.

Cassini also detected complex organic molecules within the rings that are raining down on to Saturn, an electric current connecting the rings to the atmosphere and a previously unknown radiation belt around the planet.

Perhaps one of the most intriguing results was the finding that Saturn's magnetic field is almost completely aligned with its rotational axis. This is unlike any other known magnetic field in the solar system – including Earth's – and initially caused problems for *Cassini* scientists attempting to measure the length of a day on Saturn. Usually, scientists observe how a magnetic field swings around as a planet rotates and gauge how long it takes to complete one spin. Given Saturn's magnetic field alignment, this was not possible. But the *Cassini* team were instead able to observe waves

The woman who made Earth smile

When it came to selecting *Cassini*'s imaging team leader, Carolyn Porco must have been an obvious choice. Porco wrote her thesis on *Voyager* data of Saturn's rings. Her work revealed that spokes in the rings varied in intensity and number, and that these variations were linked to bursts of radio waves emanating from the planet's magnetic field.

She was then invited to join *Voyager*'s imaging team, where she led a group responsible for observations of Neptune's rings, and later took up her post on the *Cassini* mission. Her team gave the world beautiful images of Saturn and its moons, including those incredible views of plumes erupting through the icy crust of Enceladus.

Porco had collaborated with Carl Sagan on *Voyager*'s Pale Blue Dot image (see page 186), and took the opportunity to do something similar with *Cassini*. On 19 July 2013, the spacecraft turned to photograph Earth, and Porco had encouraged people across the planet to smile together at the same time; a means to connect humanity and a reminder of our fortune at being alive on a small blue planet among the dark vacuum of the cosmos. She called the image 'The Day the Earth Smiled'. For her contribution to planetary science, Asteroid (7231) Porco was named in her honour.

in the planet's ring material caused by oscillations in its gravity field. The frequency of these oscillations enabled mission scientists to narrow the length of Saturn's day down to ten hours, thirty-three minutes and thirty-eight seconds.

The spacecraft also provided amazing views of the intriguing hexagon-shaped jet stream at Saturn's north pole, and was able to observe a 200-day storm that erupted on the planet late 2010, extending 15,000 kilometres north to south.

Saturn's icy moon, Enceladus, is thought to have a subsurface ocean beneath its frozen crust, and *Cassini* made a series of close dives that saw it fly through plumes of gas and ice erupting from below the surface. Analysis revealed the presence of hydrogen, carbon dioxide, methane and ammonia in the plumes, suggesting that the ocean of Enceladus may be able to sustain some form of life.

One of the last stages of the mission was the Grand Finale, which saw *Cassini* undertake twenty-two daring dives through the gap between the planet's rings and its cloud tops, gathering data along the way. The Grand Finale complete, *Cassini*'s time was almost up, but given the potentially habitable environments of Enceladus and Titan, mission scientists couldn't risk *Cassini* crashing on to the moons and contaminating them. On 17 September 2017, the spacecraft performed a controlled descent into Saturn's atmosphere, sending back images right up until the point it was lost for ever. After thirteen years studying the planet, *Cassini* had reached its ultimate destination, but data from the mission is set to yield even more discoveries in decades to come.

MISSION TO THE SUN

The star that burns so brightly at the centre of our solar system is still something of a mystery. We know that it is a hot ball of glowing gases, that life on Earth wouldn't exist without it, and that one day it will swallow up this planet. (Don't worry – we've still got around 5 billion years before this happens.) What we don't know is why the sun's atmosphere – the corona – is so much hotter than its surface. The corona is a searing 3,000,000 degrees Celsius, while the surface is a mere 6,000 degrees Celsius. This doesn't make sense – further away from the heat source should be cooler, not hotter. It just shouldn't happen. But it does.

Mystery number two is how solar flares occur. When electrified gas, known as plasma, is heated to extremely high temperatures, it shoots out in the form of solar flares, streaming across space as the solar wind. But how it escapes the sun's powerful gravity baffles even the brightest brains.

The only way to find out is to go there. This might sound like a crazy idea, but NASA's *Parker Solar Probe* has been designed to withstand the toasty temperatures. The special thermal protection system is a heat shield made up of two plates separated by just over 11 centimetres of carbon foam. On the outside temperatures will reach a brutal 1,377 degrees Celsius, while inside it will be a comfortable 21 degrees Celsius.

The Carrington Event

In September 1859, the worst storm in history hit. But this was no mega-hurricane. This was a solar storm in space. British astronomer Richard Carrington was doing what he normally did on a clear day – peering through his telescope at the sun from the comfort of his private observatory, skilfully drawing any sunspots that he could see. Suddenly, two white lights flashed across the sunspots and ballooned into kidney-like shapes. Then gradually, over the course of five minutes, they disappeared. At dawn the next day, multicoloured lights painted the sky in reds, greens and purples all around the world – even as far south as the equator. It was Carrington who first realized that these glowing aurorae were the result of the solar flares he had spotted erupting from the sun.

The solar storm was so violent that the aurorae-induced electric currents caused sparks to leap from telegraph equipment and even set some on fire.

Launched in 2018, the *Parker Solar Probe* uses the gravity of Venus during flybys to slingshot it into ever closer orbits around the sun. Never before has a spacecraft ventured this close to the sun, diving in and out of its corona. The mission aims to discover more about the solar wind, with the purpose of protecting technologies on Earth.

Earth is enveloped in a protective magnetic shield – the magnetosphere – which buffers the planet from the solar wind as it streams across space. Around the poles, the magnetic field can be distorted by the solar wind, allowing charged particles to sneak through the protective layer, creating stunning aurorae – the Northern and Southern lights.

The beauty of the aurorae detracts from the looming menace. Every so often, a large solar storm hits Earth, smashing into the magnetosphere and wreaking havoc with electrical technology in orbit and on the ground. It's been estimated that a huge solar storm could cause $2 trillion damage in the US alone and cut the power on the US eastern seaboard for a year.

Currently, we know around sixty minutes before a solar storm is going to hit. Understanding more about the corona and solar flares could increase the warning time to one or two days.

NASA's results from the *Parker Solar Probe* will be shared with ESA, who also have a mission to the sun planned, due to launch in 2020. The *Solar Orbiter* won't go as close to the sun as *Parker*, but will stay at the same orbiting distance for a number of years. Using on board telescopes it will look directly at the star to measure surface gas densities, temperatures and the magnetic field, as well as the solar wind. Sharing the results from both spacecraft will create a complete picture for scientists.

These missions are venturing where no craft has gone before, exploring new frontiers and pushing technology to its limits. But, if successful, they look set to reveal closely guarded secrets about our star and help protect Planet Earth for years to come.

GEDI MISSION

December 2018. The huge robotic arm of the International Space Station flexes at the 'elbow', manoeuvring into position. Its 'wrist' rolls and pitches, then locks on to the cargo inside the trunk of the visiting spacecraft's capsule. Slowly the arm pulls out an instrument, before sliding along the mobile base system towards its target – the Japanese Experiment Module-Exposed Facility (JEM-EF). The arm then spends the next few hours attaching the instrument to the outside of the space station and hooking up the power, coolant and communication systems. But it will be another few weeks of checks before it is ready to begin collecting data.

The instrument is the Global Ecosystem Dynamics Investigation, aka GEDI (pronounced 'Jedi'). Launched on 5 December 2018 from Cape Canaveral in Florida aboard the Dragon capsule of SpaceX's *Falcon 9* rocket, it is the first space-borne laser designed to peer down on Earth and measure the structure of the planet's tropical and temperate forests in high-resolution 3D. Its aim: to assess how much carbon is stored in the vegetation, and the effect that deforestation and replanting has on these 'carbon sinks', but also on biodiversity.

Forests cover around 30 per cent of the land area on our planet. Yet they are being chopped down at an alarming rate. For example, around 17 per cent of the Amazon has been lost in the last fifty years, mainly to clear land for cattle ranching.

Forests are like the lungs of the planet, soaking up carbon dioxide from the atmosphere and pumping out oxygen. Carbon makes up about 50 per cent of a tree's biomass. So when forest is chopped down, there are less trees to trap carbon – meaning that there is more of it in the atmosphere, ultimately warming the planet in a process known as the greenhouse effect.

The greenhouse effect

Without the greenhouse effect, Earth would be a frozen wasteland – a bit like Mars. Our planet needs this natural phenomenon to enable life to prosper. Yet too much of a good thing can be dangerous, and human activities are being blamed for increasing global warming.

About 30 per cent of the sun's energy is reflected off Earth's surface and back into space. But the remainder gets trapped on Earth, absorbed by greenhouse gases in the atmosphere, such as carbon dioxide. Deforestation and burning fossil fuels contribute to more carbon dioxide in the atmosphere, which in turn causes more global warming.

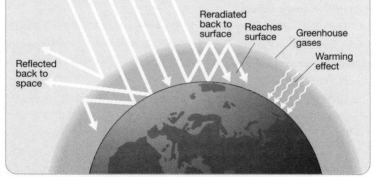

Scientists have been studying the link between deforestation and global warming for decades. But there is uncertainty about exactly how much carbon is emitted and sequestered in forests. We know that young, rapidly growing trees absorb carbon faster than mature forests. But most research on deforestation has been carried out on relatively small areas. GEDI provides the opportunity to do a large-scale assessment on the whole planet.

The instrument will also look at the canopy structure of forests – in other words, how leaves and branches are arranged. In the last three decades, species living in tropical forests have fallen by 50 per cent. Understanding how human activity impacts canopy structure will help protect other species from habitat loss and potential extinction.

GEDI is like the laser version of radar. It fires pulses of laser light at Earth and then its telescope analyses the energy reflected off vegetation, such as branches and leaves, at different heights off the ground. Using GPS, it works out its position in orbit relative to Earth's surface while star trackers give the orientation of the instrument. All of this provides detailed information about the structure of the forest canopy. The impressive thing about GEDI is that it can penetrate dense canopies, measure whole trees and accurately detect the ground on steep terrain.

The data collected by GEDI over the next couple of years should provide crucial information for scientists to understand the impact of deforestation and habitat loss. And when SpaceX's *Falcon 9* returns to collect GEDI at the end of its two-year mission, the hope is that it'll give us a better solution to protect Planet Earth from severe climate change.

PART 5

ADVENTURES YET TO COME

While humans have ventured far and wide, there are still pockets of land, ocean depths and cosmic corners that have yet to be explored. Only through tackling these challenging terrains, mysterious waters and alien worlds will we discover more about where we came from and how to steer our future. Every great adventure starts with vision, risk-taking and courage to challenge science as we know it and explore new frontiers.

WHAT LIES BENEATH ANTARCTICA

Life at Vostok Research Station is brutal. The base holds the record for the coldest temperature anywhere on the planet: a bone-chilling −89 degrees Celsius. Drop your glove and you will lose your fingers. Yet, for some of the year, the site is home to a hardy bunch of scientists. Run by Russian researchers, their work has been focused on finding out what lurks beneath their feet.

Trapped under more than 3.7 kilometres of ice is Lake Vostok – the largest of almost 400 sub-glacial lakes in Antarctica. At 230 kilometres long and 50 kilometres wide, the vast body of water would take a week to walk from end to end. Frozen over for the last 15 million years, its contents have been cut off from the rest of the planet. Its only interaction with the outside world is melt water filtering down from the layer of ice above.

The lake was first discovered by an eagle-eyed Russian pilot back in the 1960s. But he had no idea what the expansive depression in the ice could be. It wasn't until the early 1990s that scientists realized that a lake lay buried beneath the surface. Using radar, seismographs and satellite images, they built up a map of the enormous body of water below.

Despite the bitter temperatures, it is thought that geothermal heat warms the water to around −3 degrees Celsius, and then the pressure of the thick blanket of ice above prevents the lake from freezing up.

Life is thought to exist in its chilly depths. The combination of cold and geothermal heat, pressure, pitch-black darkness and minimal nutrients mean any life would have to be extremely tough.

But so-called 'extremophiles' do exist in other remote corners of the planet, where other creatures struggle to survive.

Water bears

As the name suggests, 'extremophiles' are hardy organisms that can survive in extreme environments. Perhaps most famous of all is the tardigrade, also known as a 'water bear'. This microscopic organism, with its plump body and stumpy legs, can cope with temperatures ranging from −272 to +150 degrees Celsius, and can live without water for years. Tests by the European Space Agency (ESA) have shown that they can also survive harsh radiation and even the vacuum of space. Their secret: to shut down all vital functions and live in a suspended state until better times come along.

Carcasses of tardigrades have been discovered in another Antarctic lake. Starting in December 2018, the Subglacial Antarctic Lakes Scientific Access (SALSA) project spent a month drilling over 1,200 metres down into Mercer Lake. The researchers think the tardigrades may have lived in ponds and streams around 50 kilometres away, thought to have existed when Antarctica was warmer, either in the past 10,000 years or 120,000 years ago. But no one knows how the creatures made it to Mercer Lake. Carbon dating and DNA analysis may provide the answer.

So far, scientists have drilled down to the roof of Lake Vostok. Samples from the accretion ice above it have revealed DNA from microbes, such as bacteria and fungi. The next step will be to drill right through to the water itself. But the big challenge will be ensuring the pristine environment does not become contaminated by life from above, as we have seen on other parts of the planet how the introduction of alien species can decimate native populations. Once that protective barrier is breached, there will be no going back.

Aside from the tantalizing prospect of possibly discovering endemic species that are completely unique to Lake Vostok, the research could also give us some clues as to whether life could survive on other planets, such as inside Mars' ice cap or underneath the icy surface of Jupiter's moon Europa.

THE LANDS THAT TIME FORGOT

In this modern world, where it's difficult to get truly off-the-beaten-track and out of Wi-Fi signal, few areas on the planet remain uncharted. Yet around 70 per cent of Papua New Guinea (PNG) is believed to be unexplored – the dense rainforest and steep, rugged mountains are a natural deterrent.

Of course, this means unexplored by the Western world. Much of that land has been lived on by local tribes for thousands of years. But some of those tribes have never had contact with the outside world. Others have, and the visitors paid the price – cannibalism was once common in parts of PNG. Reputedly this is no longer the case. Geographic barriers have kept communities isolated from one another, making PNG the most linguistically diverse place on Earth, with nearly 850 languages. Most of PNG's population hug the coastal lowlands, where fishing and trade flourish. But the remote highlands of dense rainforest, rugged mountains, deep gorges and fiery volcanoes are home to vibrant cultures and rich wildlife, including forty-two different species of birds of paradise. Indeed, this area, which covers less than 1 per cent of the world's landmass, has around 10 per cent of the world's vertebrates and 7 per cent of the world's higher plants.

A number of PNG species hold world records: the red-breasted pygmy parrot (8 centimetres long) is the smallest on the planet; the crocodile monitor (2.4 metres long) is the longest lizard; and the Queen Alexandra's birdwing (with a wingspan of up to 28 centimetres) is the world's largest butterfly.

PNG is also home to some bizarre beasts. The turkey-sized megapode bird has a unique and unusual strategy for rearing its young. Instead of using its own body heat to incubate the eggs, it digs deep into volcanic ash and uses the warmth of the volcano to incubate them.

In recent years, scientists and TV crews have explored deeper into the highlands. A recent scientific expedition unearthed dozens of previously unidentified species, including a giant woolly rat the size of a large cat. Another expedition tracked the Wondiwoi tree kangaroo, which was thought to have gone extinct almost a century ago. This close relative of ground-dwelling kangaroos and wallabies

Masta Mick

As recently as the twentieth century, the highlands of PNG were thought to be uninhabited by humans, being too cold for tropical people. But a colourful explorer, Michael James Leahy, changed all that. Mick was born in Queensland, Australia, and at the age of twenty-five packed in his regular job and headed for PNG, where he'd heard about a gold strike. Despite malaria almost killing him – and killing his dreams of striking gold – he fell in love with the country.

In 1930, he walked across the interior of PNG and was amazed by what he encountered – stunning landscapes, intriguing wildlife and curious tribes. This was the start of a lifetime of expeditions, photographing and filming PNG's rich diversity. During his travels, the cannibals never got 'Masta Mick', as he was fondly known by his PNG friends. He died of natural causes at the age of seventy-eight on a mountain top in the north-east of the country in 1979.

lives up to its name, hopping between branches and hauling itself up trunks with its muscular forearms.

Yet so much of the PNG highlands still remain unexplored. The country is one of the last remaining places on the planet with many secrets as yet untold. Future expeditions may uncover its mysteries. But these magical lands will surely challenge even the toughest of explorers.

SWIMMING IN SINKHOLES

Traipsing through the dense undergrowth are two dive buddies, carrying their tanks, camera kit and GPS devices. The pair reach a manhole-sized gap in the forest floor. Donning their wetsuits and dive kit, they attach a rope ladder to the base of a tree trunk and climb down, past ancient roots. The shaft gets narrower and narrower, until at last it opens up into an enormous cavern, almost completely filled with water. They dive down and hunt for a different tunnel that will lead them on to another cavern. Their aim is to navigate through a vast network of caves until they reach the open ocean.

This duo is part of a new breed of divers exploring the vast water-filled cave systems in the Yucatan Peninsula in Mexico. Access is either from the coast in the Gulf of Mexico or via the sinkholes, known locally as *cenotes* – from the Mayan word meaning 'water deposit'.

The *cenotes* are thought to have formed when the asteroid that wiped out the dinosaurs smashed into the peninsula. The impact vaporized everything at the surface, tearing great gashes underground, which flooded with seawater from the ocean. Over time, some of the ground subsided to form *cenotes* and a layer of freshwater gradually built up on top of the seawater.

In between the layers, clouds of toxic hydrogen sulphide form, as rotting organic matter decomposes when no oxygen is present. The gas smells like rotten eggs and is lethal if inhaled. Fortunately explorers have their protective dive gear.

In these dark submerged caverns it's hard to imagine the bright sunlight beating down on the world above. But not far overhead is a vibrant holiday destination. The heat and exotic archaeology draw in millions of tourists each year. Each of those tourists needs a bed in a hotel or hostel – some of which don't treat their sewage, which inevitably makes its way into the groundwater and down into the vast aquifer of the cave systems below. Protecting the unique underground ecosystem is a challenge. Many of the divers are scientists intent on finding evidence to show why the cave systems are so ecologically and historically important.

The Ik Kil *cenote* in Mexico

In 2018, divers from the Great Maya Aquifer Project discovered a link between two huge underwater caverns. Combined they form a vast 350-kilometre-long network – the largest in the world. Submerged in the depths are species previously unknown to science, numerous ancient Mayan artefacts and remains, and a 12,000-year-old human skeleton – the oldest one found in the Americas.

Exploration of these cave systems began only in the 1980s. Explorers would hire small single-engine planes and fly over the dense jungle, hunting for *cenotes*. When they spotted one, they reportedly dropped a roll of toilet paper to mark the spot, later retrieving it on foot, dive gear at the ready.

Since then, many incredible cave systems have been discovered. But, while divers are gradually connecting the dots of the *cenotes* by traversing the watery caverns, so many are yet to be explored. Who knows what other treasures may lie waiting to be discovered in the submerged labyrinth of the Yucatan.

ASTEROID IMPACT MISSION

Smashing into the Yucatan Peninsula 66 million years ago, at thousands of kilometres per hour, the Chicxulub impactor sounded the death knell for the dinosaurs. Travelling about twenty times faster than a speeding bullet, this asteroid was between 10 and 15 kilometres wide and its impact generated a force more than 1 billion times greater than the atomic bomb dropped on Hiroshima, vaporizing the immediate area. Thick dust rose into the atmosphere. Over the next few weeks, the dust engulfed the planet, blocking out the sun – signalling the end for most of life on Earth.

Fortunately for us humans, some tiny mammalian ancestors managed to survive this Armageddon. And the good news is that now we should be technologically advanced enough to fend off an asteroid impact in the future. NASA and the European Space Agency (ESA) have been working together in a bid to save humanity from a catastrophic asteroid impact. The Asteroid Intercept and Deflection Assessment (AIDA) is the first-ever attempt to knock an asteroid off course. The ambitious programme will be rolled out in three stages.

Firstly, in 2021, NASA will launch the Double Asteroid Redirection Test (DART) spacecraft. It will head for Didymos, an asteroid whose orbit gets to within 10 million kilometres of Earth. DART's actual target is Didymoon – the nickname given to the 170-kilometre-long lump of rock that orbits the asteroid. Smashing the 100-kilo spacecraft into Didymoon at about 6 kilometres per second (around nine times faster than a bullet) will change the rock's speed by just a few millimetres per second, which should be enough to affect the speed that it orbits around the asteroid.

The second stage will be carried out by a miniaturized satellite, nicknamed Selfiesat. Launched by DART just before impact, this cereal-packet-sized satellite, which was made by the Italian Space Agency, will snap photos of the event to provide a basic understanding of how successful the mission has been. Then we'll have to wait until 2026 for the final stage, when ESA's Hera spacecraft will arrive in orbit, to get a more detailed picture. The key aim will be to work out the mass of the moon, as that will indicate the effect of DART's impact and whether the mission was successful.

Currently, space agencies have telescopes scanning the skies for dangerous-looking asteroids. Any larger than 10 kilometres in diameter are considered powerful enough to destroy life on Earth. The location is known of around 90 per cent of the ones that could cause extinction. If one is spotted, the key is to find out everything we can about it – it's size, shape, density and what it's made of, as all of this affects how we deal with it. That way we can decide the best course of action.

If we spot one early enough, then a gentle nudge should be sufficient to knock it off course. But if we catch it a bit late, we might have to resort to using a nuclear bomb. The shockwave from detonating a bomb near an asteroid might be enough to deflect it off course. But a better option might be to plant a bomb below the asteroid surface, blowing it up into smaller pieces. Although if those pieces don't burn up as they enter Earth's atmosphere, they might end up raining down on our planet, causing even more havoc.

Our best bet is to research all the options, so that we're prepared for the worst-case scenario. By the end of the AIDA mission, we should know more about whether we can rely on the impactor method to knock a threatening asteroid off course. Indeed, AIDA may end up being our best insurance policy for Planet Earth.

EXPLORING EUROPA

Europa is just one of Jupiter's seventy-nine known moons, and yet it is one of the most intriguing. Its elliptical orbit means its nearside feels more of the strength of Jupiter's gravity, causing tides that stretch and flex the moon, ripping great gashes in its surface. The surface is frozen, covered with a layer of ice up to 25 kilometres thick. But scientists think that beneath the outer layer lies a vast salty ocean, 60 to 150 kilometres deep. This would mean that, although Europa is one-fourth the diameter of Earth, its ocean could hold twice as much water.

The tantalizing prospect that water exists comes from evidence that Europa may be venting plumes of water vapour above its icy shell. Back in the 1990s, NASA's *Galileo* spacecraft was on a tour of the solar system. One target was Jupiter and its moons. Data collected by the spacecraft in 1997 has recently been re-analysed. Temporary magnetic anomalies, which baffled scientists at the time, now hint of water plumes. Indeed, UV images captured by the Hubble Space Telescope in 2012 seemed to suggest jets of water were erupting from the surface.

Other intriguing features are also getting scientists excited. On *Galileo*'s flyby, the spacecraft spotted numerous craters scattered across the moon, suggesting that the surface is relatively young – 40 to 90 million years old – a mere blip in the story of the solar system. If this is the case, then something must be re-paving the surface, as Jupiter's largest moons (Io, Europa, Ganymede, and Callisto) are thought to have formed around 4.5 billion years ago from material left over after Jupiter condensed from the initial cloud of gas and dust surrounding the sun. Volcanic activity could be responsible for the re-paving. And, if that's the case, then hydrothermal activity on a seafloor could be firing nutrients into an ocean. Water plus nutrients equals the potential for life. Europa beckons.

A new mission is on the horizon to investigate the moon for signs of life. Due to launch in the next few years, NASA's Europa Clipper will carry out forty-five flybys, diving to within just 25 kilometres of the moon's surface – plenty close enough to pass through any water plumes which are thought to be fired up to 160 kilometres into the atmosphere. Kitted out with all sorts of hi-tech devices to probe below the moon's surface, Clipper hopes to get an answer to whether life exists. Ice-penetrating radar will work out the exact thickness of the moon's icy shell and hunt for the proposed subsurface ocean, while a magnetometer will calculate the strength and direction of its magnetic field, so scientists can calculate its exact depth and salinity if one does exist.

Scientists are hopeful that a watery world does lie buried beneath the moon's surface. If so, this could be the start of an exciting new era in the hunt for alien life.

A vision of hell

One of Jupiter's other moons, Io, is the most volcanically active spot in the solar system. With hundreds of active volcanoes, its surface is like a vision of hell. Mountains – some taller than Everest – are interspersed by fiery volcanoes, which shoot lava and plumes of sulphur and sulphur dioxide many kilometres into the air. Lakes of molten silicate lava pool on the surface, painting it various colours of the rainbow.

This fiery action is caused by so-called 'tidal heating'. Io is trapped in a tug-of-war between Jupiter's massive gravity and the other main moons – Europa, Ganymede and Callisto. All this pushing and pulling heats the moon's core, creating this fascinating fireball.

EYE IN THE SKY

After a thirty-minute ride into space, the capsule detaches from its launch vehicle. Guided by remote control, over the course of two weeks the space telescope gradually takes shape – deploying its antennae, then the sunshield, the mirror, and finally spreading its wings. At least this is the plan for the launch of the James Webb Space Telescope (JWST), which is due to rocket into space in 2021. This complex mission has been over twenty years in the planning and construction and is one of the most challenging engineering projects ever attempted.

Over 1,200 scientists and engineers from NASA, the European Space Agency (ESA) and the Canadian Space Agency (CSA) have worked tirelessly for years to bring the JWST to life. Named after the second administrator of NASA, when the space telescope was first conceived much of its technology hadn't even been invented yet. As happened with the Apollo programme, the engineers had to come up with a number of completely new technologies never before seen on spacecraft, then rigorously test them.

No previous space telescope has had moveable mirrors, computer software to control them, or a huge sunshield the size of a tennis court. This is the largest and most advanced orbital observatory ever built.

The Hubble Space Telescope, launched in 1990, was the first space-based telescope. It broke records and stunned the world with the incredible images it captured of the cosmos. Far above Earth's atmosphere, away from light pollution, its many achievements included spotting monster black holes, shining a light on mysterious dark matter and exploring the birth of stars (and watching their death throes). But after almost three decades and covering 6.4 billion kilometres, it's time for it to make way for the next generation.

Almost 100 times more powerful, the JWST has a vast primary mirror 6.5 metres across, dwarfing that of Hubble at a mere 2.4 metres. The huge size of this mirror ensures it will capture every last possible infrared photon that falls on it. It is made from beryllium – which can be moulded yet is lightweight, strong and stiff, and is often used for making supersonic planes and spacecraft. The mirror is then coated in a very thin layer of gold, which improves the mirror's reflection of infrared light – the main wavelength of light this telescope will observe.

The telescope support structure is built using a lightweight carbon-composite material, which is revolutionary because it can keep its rigid shape to 1/10,000th of a human hair. Keeping the telescope very cool is also vital to ensure it doesn't glow with heat, which would obscure the view of its instruments. Hence the enormous sunshield that acts like a vast parasol, protecting the telescope's mirrors from the heat of the sun.

All of this incredible engineering will allow the JWST to peer way back into the past to the first light of the universe, watch galaxies collide, see stars and exoplanets being born, and probe the many mysteries of the universe.

In the future, when it stares out into the depths of space from its orbit around the sun, 1.5 million kilometres from Earth, the JWST will hopefully find clues about where we came from, how this planet we live on formed, and where else life could be lurking in the cosmos.

MANNED MISSION TO MARS

Mars has roughly one-third the gravity of Earth, a thin atmosphere made up mostly of carbon dioxide, and is bombarded by lethal radiation. So the thought of living on Mars seems fairly unappealing. But space agencies around the world have set their sights on humans setting foot on the Red Planet within the next few decades.

There are currently three main projects battling it out in this new Space Race. NASA is testing the *Orion* spacecraft, with the final goal of one day sending astronauts to Mars, while a number of former NASA and ESA employees have banded together to form the privately run project Mars One. And Elon Musk, founder of PayPal and Tesla, is developing the next iteration of SpaceX's reusable spacecraft – BFR – with the hope of manned missions to Mars in the next decade. The race is on.

The human body on Mars

From astronauts living on the International Space Station, we know that in low-gravity environments bone and muscle waste away, the heart deconditions, the immune system gets suppressed and the lack of red blood cells can make astronauts anaemic. To keep humans in peak condition, scientists are proposing some ingenious solutions to combat low gravity. Astronauts could stand in a so-called short-arm centrifuge that would whizz them around, providing their daily dose of artificial gravity. Alternatively, they could wear 'skinsuits' designed to compress the body slightly, ensuring it is exposed to the equivalent of 1 g (Earth's gravity) at all times.

Lethal radiation is another huge challenge to combat. Earth is protected by a thick atmosphere, as well as a magnetic shield that deflects harmful rays that would otherwise damage DNA and cause mutations, potentially creating tumours. No such thing exists around the Red Planet. A Mars base would need to be designed with radiation shielding – or maybe drugs will be developed to mop up any harmful atoms in the body, known as 'free radicals', which develop as a result of radiation exposure.

The journey to Mars would take between six to eight months, depending on the timing of the trip. Roughly every two years, Mars is at its closest point – 55 million kilometres from Earth, which is still 9,800 times the distance between London and New York. Such a distance inevitably throws up many challenges – not least landing a crew on the Martian surface. NASA estimates that a six-person mission would need a 40,000-kilo spacecraft. That's some serious weight to land on the Red Planet, particularly if you compare it to the heaviest load to date, which was 1,000 kilos when the *Curiosity* rover touched down (see page 211). As Elon Musk has pointed out, the first astronauts on Mars missions would be risking their lives. 'It kind of reads like Shackleton's ad for Antarctic explorers. Difficult, dangerous, good chance you'll die. Excitement for those who survive.'

Indeed, Mars is home to some of the most incredible sights in the solar system, such as the vast canyon Valles Marineris and the super-volcano Olympus Mons. At 4,000 kilometres long and 7 kilometres deep, Valles Marineris would swallow the Grand Canyon (446 kilometres long and 1.6 kilometres deep), while Olympus Mons is the largest known volcano in the solar system – at 25 kilometres high and 624 kilometres in diameter it would dwarf the shield volcano Mauna Loa (120 kilometres across) in Hawaii. Maybe one day Mars colonists will set off on expeditions to travel the length of Valles Marineris on foot or to conquer the summit of Olympus Mons.

First though, early colonists would need to build bases to live in, grow food, produce energy and create oxygen. Life on Mars would not be easy – full of challenges and hazards. But, of course, potential discoveries would have a profound effect on future generations – proving that if we can survive on Mars, humans might one day be able to live further afield, beyond the confines of our solar system.

MINING MERCURY

In the future, if we're looking to voyage deep into the cosmos, Mercury would be a good initial destination to kick-start the journey. If you were standing on the surface of Mercury, the sun would look twice as big in the sky as on Earth. After all, Mercury is the closest planet to our star. Even at its furthest point from the sun, it is an average distance of 58 million kilometres away, compared to Earth at 152,100,000 kilometres.

Being so close to our star means there's plenty of sunlight beating down on the rocky planet and therefore plenty of potential for the planet to capture solar energy. On Mercury you'd need just 1 square metre of solar panels, compared to 6 square metres on Earth, to produce the same amount of power.

Solar sails are one propulsion method currently being researched by space agencies from Tokyo to Houston. When sunlight hits a reflecting surface, a pressure builds up as the light particles rebound from the surface and push the object in the opposite direction. On Earth, an 800-metre-wide sail would receive five Newtons of light-pressure. On Mercury you'd need a sail only half that size to create the same pressure. And, on a trip to the far-flung reaches of the solar system, you'd be better off journeying to Mercury first to give an initial boost to the spacecraft. But a trip to Mercury wouldn't be without its challenges.

Studying the innermost planet from Earth is extremely tricky as it is always too close to the sun in the sky. But NASA's *MESSENGER* spacecraft, launched in 2004, orbited Mercury between 2011 and 2015, returning a wealth of data which gave us a whole new insight into this intriguing planet.

We now know that Mercury started off life as a larger planet with an iron-nickel core and rocky mantle. A cataclysmic collision with another celestial object stripped the mantle, leaving behind a smaller yet still very hot planet. As it cooled, it shrank, shrivelling up like an apple past its prime, which created wrinkles on the planet's surface, known as 'rupes'.

In the daytime, Mercury's surface is hot enough to melt lead. At night, however, the temperature drops to a chilly −200 degrees Celsius, as its thin atmosphere doesn't trap any warmth. Extremes like this would understandably put off many an intrepid explorer. But the potential riches buried in this hostile planet are intriguing.

What's left of the mantle is rich in resources, such as heavy metals like aluminium and titanium, as well as oxygen, calcium, magnesium and potassium. With plenty of solar energy to power mining operations, Mercury could be the future 'gold mine' of the solar system.

In 2018, ESA and the Japan Aerospace Exploration Agency jointly launched the *BepiColombo* spacecraft with the aim of getting up close and personal with Mercury. The craft is due to reach the planet in late 2025. The mission aim is to find out more about the composition of its atmosphere, its large core, polar ice, mysterious magnetic field, and how it interacts with the solar wind (a stream of plasma and particles from the sun).

We'll have to wait and see what secrets *BepiColombo* reveals. But, one day, hardy explorers may venture to the inhospitable planet in search of its treasures – and a ticket out of the solar system.

Space law

As the reality of space mining draws ever closer, the need for tighter regulation grows. The Outer Space Treaty (OST) is over fifty years old. Drawn up in 1967, the pact describes space as 'the province of all mankind' and forbids any state from colonizing any object in space or using it for military purposes. So, no country can own any planet, asteroid or any other celestial body, regardless of whether they plant a flag there. But the OST lacks detail, including any explicit mention of mining. And some experts foresee future controversy as space belongs to everyone, hence the resources belong to everyone.

MOON BASE

'Now, let's get off. Forget the camera.' These are thought to be the last words that were spoken on the moon. The date was 14 December 1972. It was the end of an era. As the *Apollo 17* crew fired up the engine and lifted off the lunar surface, the program that had inspired the Space Race and made Neil Armstrong and Buzz Aldrin household names drew to a close. Since then, only robots have roamed the surface of our nearest lunar neighbour. But, almost five decades on, that could be about to change.

ESA Director General Johann-Dietrich Woerner wants to pool the expertise of space agencies around the globe to build a permanent international space station on the moon. It's an ambitious project. The cost of firing even one kilo of material into space is $10,000, so ferrying everything needed for a whole base would be prohibitively expensive. Instead, the plan is to use as many local resources as possible.

Architects Foster & Partners have been in discussions with ESA about possible designs. One idea is for a robot to inflate a temporary scaffold and then 3D print a permanent domed structure over that using lunar soil, known as regolith. Meanwhile, NASA has been working with Bigelow Aerospace to use a standalone inflatable pod.

Any design would need to protect residents from lethal radiation. Earth is enveloped in a thick atmosphere and magnetic shield that deflects harmful rays that damages DNA. As the moon has no such protection, a lunar base would need to have very thick walls – at least a couple of metres in diameter to soak up the radiation.

Local resources would also dictate where the base would be located. Water ice exists at both lunar poles, which would be potential drinking water for residents, as well as a way of getting hold of oxygen by splitting H_2O. The south pole seems like the best bet, as temperatures are not as extreme and there's plenty of daylight – useful for powering solar panels.

But the big question is why is it worth going back to the moon? There are a number of reasons. Firstly, it is resource rich. Secondly, the far side of the moon is also a great site for telescopes – an optical telescope would have an unrivalled view of our galaxy, while a radio telescope would be protected from the constant hum of human-made signals and could peer deep into the cosmos. But, crucially, the moon would also be an important stepping stone and testing ground on the quest for a manned mission to Mars.

Only twelve humans have ever set foot on the moon. This small number is surprising, given it's our closest neighbour. But within the next decade, humans may once again take giant leaps for humankind upon the lunar surface.

Exploring the far side of the moon

In January 2019, the Chinese Chang'e-4 probe landed on the far side of the moon, where no human-made device had ever been before. Packed with instruments, it set about recording all sorts of data: listening to radio signals from space, monitoring radiation strength, and studying the solar wind (a stream of plasma and particles from the sun).

On board was the Yutu-2 rover, which analysed the lunar surface for valuable minerals, such as helium-3 – a potentially useful fuel source. Also on board were biological experiments in order to see how organic matter, such as fruit-fly eggs and various seeds, coped with the extremes of space. They didn't last long, but cotton, rape and potato seeds became the first plants ever to germinate on another planet. The hope is that one day a moon colony could grow food and cotton for clothes.

MISSION TO HELL

The view beneath the thick blanket of cloud was astounding. The rocky surface was virtually blemish-free, except for one huge crater scarring the flat plain. The year was 1990 – and this was the first-ever glimpse of the surface of Venus. Over the following months and years, as the *Magellan* spacecraft captured image after image using radar mapping, a vision of hell began to emerge – and scientists started to realize that Venus was unlike any other planet in the solar system.

Most rocky planets are scarred by craters caused by asteroid impacts. But, while Venus has high volcanic mountains and vast ridged plateaus, it lacks many craters – suggesting it has been resurfaced by recent volcanism. And a subsequent mission has found hints that lava may still be erupting today. Thermal imaging by ESA's Venus Express probe, which orbited Venus from 2006 to 2014, showed hot patches that warmed and cooled over time, suggesting they might be lava lakes bubbling up from beneath the surface.

Volcanism fires carbon dioxide into the atmosphere. But, unlike on Earth where some carbon gets locked away in sediments and then dragged deep underground at subduction zones (see page 52), Venus doesn't seem to have plate tectonics. With nowhere to go, carbon dioxide builds up in the atmosphere, trapping the sun's heat. This is how the so-called 'greenhouse effect' works.

If we want to get an idea of what might happen to Earth if global warming gets too bad, Venus is a good place to look. Scientists think that the planet suffered what's known as a 'runaway greenhouse effect' around 3 to 4 billion years ago. If a planet absorbs more energy from the sun than it can radiate back to space then it gets hotter and hotter, until its oceans boil away.

Soon after the solar system formed around 4.6 billion years

ago, the rocky planets Venus, Earth and Mars most likely all had water. But, over time, while Earth became a paradise for life, Venus transformed into hell.

Despite being roughly the same size as Earth and similar in structure, Venus is worlds apart in many ways. Atmospheric pressure is ninety times what exists at sea level on Earth – and crushed the first probes that tried to land. Surface temperatures are double those found in a kitchen oven – hot enough to melt lead.

Scientists believe that studying Venus is crucial to understanding our own changing climate and how we can ensure a runaway greenhouse effect doesn't make our own planet inhabitable in years to come.

Future missions to Venus are on the drawing board, with all sorts of plans for orbiters, balloons and aerial vehicles. Let's hope at least some of them do take off, as further exploring our toxic twin might just save our planet.

THE NEW GOLD RUSH

Intrepid explorers, battling the elements, braving extremes, on the hunt for treasures that will bring untold riches. This could be a scene from the Wild West, where the lucky few survive the long, arduous trip across the North American continent to lands rich in gold. But this is not the Californian gold rush. This is the future, where hardy astronauts journey across the solar system to mine other worlds for their natural resources, such as water, minerals and precious metals.

Water will be vital for any future manned space missions, while being a good way to cool spacecraft systems as well. It could also be used as a fuel if split into hydrogen and oxygen. But firing a 450-gram bottle of water into orbit currently costs about £2,000, so mining it in space for off-Earth colonies would be far cheaper once the infrastructure is in place.

Mining space for precious metals will also be important in the future. Precious metals exist in everything from our electronic gadgets to renewable technologies, such as solar panels, wind turbines and electric-car batteries. Yet resources on Earth are becoming harder to come by. Miners are having to dig ever deeper and even hunt for them at the bottom of the ocean. This is because Earth's gravity caused precious metals to be dragged down towards the core, meaning they are relatively rare in the crust. But, as asteroids have relatively small masses and hence weaker gravity, precious metals are distributed more evenly throughout, and so more exist closer to the surface.

Ranging in size from a few metres wide to several hundred kilometres across, an asteroid just one kilometre in diameter could hold billions of dollars worth of resources. Indeed, meteorites

How asteroids formed

Around 4.6 billion years ago, the solar system was a dangerous place. A wispy cloud of dust and gas collapsed in on itself, creating a spinning disc, with a central proto-star. Over time, bits of the swirling mass started to clump together, as ever larger and larger pieces smashed into one another, congealing into vast planets and catapulting smaller bodies into space. What remained were a number of planets orbiting the sun and other rocky bodies such as moons and asteroids.

Untouched by the forces that moulded planets like Earth, for billions of years asteroids have remained unchanged. They are like time capsules – crack them open and they could reveal the secrets of the early solar system, including how the planets, moons and other celestial bodies formed.

contain around five times as much gold as on Earth – and about ten times as much of extremely rare metals, such as osmium.

For this new band of gold hunters, the good news is that taking off and landing on an asteroid doesn't use that much energy, because of the weak gravity. The tricky bit is getting both humans and mining equipment there.

Most asteroids lie in the so-called 'asteroid belt' between Mars and Jupiter, although some are closer to home. These Near-Earth Asteroids (NEA) are easier targets to reach, requiring less fuel to get there, but they may not be as resource-rich. Scientists can work out the size of an asteroid by the amount of heat it emits using infrared telescopes, such as the Spitzer Space Telescope, which orbits the sun, as well as an asteroid's composition by measuring the amount

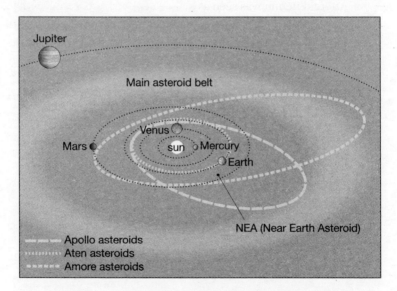

Miners will target Near Earth Asteroids as less fuel will be needed to reach them

of sunlight reflected from its surface (albedo). So it's possible to know if an asteroid is likely to be rich in metals or carbon.

The best way to find out exactly what an asteroid is made of is, of course, to journey there and collect a sample. Back in 2010, the Japanese Aerospace Exploration Agency's (JAXA) *Hayabusa* mission returned a small sample from the asteroid Itokawa. While it gave invaluable insight into the asteroid's composition, the sample was mixed with contaminant particles from the spacecraft.

Two new sample-return missions are underway. JAXA's next iteration, *Hayabusa2*, launched in 2014, while NASA's *OSIRIS-REx* took off in 2016. Both have successfully rendezvoused with their respective asteroids – Ryugu and Bennu – and are carrying out surveys before returning home, hopefully with pristine rock samples (see page 157).

Asteroid Bennu was seen as a good target by NASA for a number of reasons: it is relatively close to Earth; it is not too small and so doesn't tumble around in space too much, which would make it hard to get samples; and it is a carbonaceous asteroid, meaning it could be rich in water and organic molecules.

While neither of these asteroids is rich in precious metals, these missions could pave the way for more adventurous operations to mine other asteroids for their treasures.

ACKNOWLEDGEMENTS

A huge thank you to Iain Todd for your help in writing this book. Thank you also to Josie Clarkson for your help with research. And to my friends and family who shared their resources and ideas about icons of scientific exploration.

PICTURE CREDITS

Page 26: Illustration from *Mémoire sur l'os hyoïde et le larynx des oiseaux, des singes et du crocodile* by Alexander von Humboldt, F. Schoell, Paris 1811

Page 48: Illustration from *Travels in West Africa* by Mary H. Kingsley, Macmillan and Co., Limited, London 1897

Page 51: Photograph from the archive of the Alfred Wegener Institute

Page 67: Photograph courtesy of Colonel John Blashford-Snell CBE and the Scientific Exploration Society / www.ses-explore.org

Page 82: Gypsum crystals of the Naica cave; Alexander Van Driessche, Wikimedia CC 3.0

Page 93: Illustration from *A Voyage to New Holland in the Year 1699* by Captain William Dampier, Third Edition, London 1729

Page 130: Photograph by Ullstein Bild via Getty Images

Page 198: Photograph of Philae lander on Comet 67P; ESA, Rosetta, MPS, OSIRIS; UPD / LAM / IAA / SSO / INTA / UPM / DASP / IDA / Navcam

Page 239: Photograph by Vadim Petrakov / Shutterstock

INDEX